PHILOSOPHY
OF
LIBRARY CLASSIFICATION

Philosophy of Library Classification

S R Ranganathan

SARADA RANGANATHAN ENDOWMENT
FOR LIBRARY SCIENCE
Bangalore-560 078

Shiyali Ramamrita Ranganathan (1892-1972)

Reprinted 1989
Reprint **2006**

ISBN: 81-7000-471-3

Rs.250/-

Published By:
Ess Ess Publications
4837/24, Ansari Road,
Darya Ganj,
New Delhi-110 002
Ph.No. 23260807, 51563444, Fax: 51563334
E-mail: info@essessreference.com
url: www.essessreference.com

For:
Sarada Ranganathan Endowment for Library Science
702, 'Upstairs',
42nd Cross, III Block,
Rajajinagar,
Bangalore-560 010.
Ph.No. 23305109
E-mail: srels@vsnl.com

Printed in India at: Printline, New Delhi

251
J0

TO
SOW
AVIAMBAL

CONTENTS

CONSPECTUS

Dr. Jean Anker invited me to write a monograph on the *Philosophy of library classification* for his series Library Research Monographs and I accepted the invitation. I now find that it has provided me with an opportunity to straighten in my own mind the principles of library classification on which I had been thinking for some years. The moment which he chose to invite me was one of crisis in my mind. My recent visit to Europe and America, which made me contact Dr. Anker himself and many other colleagues, helped me to realise the great demand which is developing in all spheres of thought — pure as well as applied — for documentation service of the most exact and exhaustive kind. It also gave me an opportunity to experience the inadequacy of the existing classificatory technique to meet that demand.

The feeling in me has been very similar to what it was when I visited the British libraries twenty-five years ago. At that time also, I experienced the inability of the then known classificatory technique to meet the demands of book-service. It was this which led to the designing of new foundations for library classification and to a comparative study leading to the enunciation of the canons and principles of the subject.

The present experience has led to the deepening of these foundations so as to take the additional load of documentation. So far it has not been possible to find a totally new foundation. All that has happened is to carry the existing foundations to a deeper level. It is on occasions like this when the foundations of a subject are re-examined and re-designed or deepened that one is led to a study of its general principles. And it is study of this kind which constitutes its philosophy.

For, the sixth meaning of philosophy recorded in the *New English dictionary* is "The study of the general principles of some particular branch of knowledge, experience or activity". Library classification is surely an activity which has become essential to all librarians who wish to make their libraries an effective agency in the exact and expeditious distribution of all recorded knowledge among the right consumers. Library classification is also an experience whose profoundness increases with the depth to which it is taken to keep step with the new formations in the field of knowledge, especially in its deeper layers. Library classification has itself become a region of knowledge which has well-defined boundaries. Its cultivation has an individuality of its own. It calls for specific methods of investigation and development. It has acquired all the features of a discipline which is entitled to be recognised as a branch of knowledge.

There are various branches of knowledge which have knowledge itself as the object of study.

Psychology is one of them. It seeks to explore what happens to the mind and in the mind in building up knowledge. Logic is another which deals with the way in which the intellect develops the impressions and experiences stored in memory and creates new impressions and experiences which add to knowledge. Epistemology deals with one aspect of the nature of the knowledge restored and stored in one's memory: its sources and validity. Ontology examines another aspect of the nature of knowledge — its reduction to the minimum number of ultimates and the reality or otherwise of the correlates of knowledge outside the knower's mind. A fifth branch concerns itself with a description and assorting of the different kinds of knowledge-formations, their interrelations and the distinctive methods of investigation used in them. This I have called the Field of Knowledge.

A sixth branch is concerned with the organisation of the specific subjects — macroscopic as well as microscopic — which are recognisable in the field of knowledge, the mode of their arrangement in a helpful order and the development of an apparatus to mechanise the recalling, preservation and restoration of the preferred order. This is called Library Classification. The philosophy of library classification has for its domain the general principles of the last-mentioned branch of knowledge concerning knowledge itself.

The first chapter is devoted to a clarification of the term "classification" and the fixing of the meaning of the term "Library classification". This clarification brings out the idea that library classification has a two-fold aspect: (1) the throwing of specific subjects in a helpful order — the older meaning of classification; and (2) the building of a system of notation to represent them in that order. It traces the evolution of the different features of such a system of notation in some of the systems of classification like the Decimal, the Universal Decimal and the Colon schemes. The concepts of Facet-Analysis, Phase-Analysis and Focus are introduced.

The second chapter presents the notational system of a library classification as an artificial language of ordinal numbers. It enumerates the chief qualities which such a language should have. It shows how classificatory language differs from a natural language in its elements, morphology, syntax, semasiology and growth. It discusses the principles involved in facetisation and the sharpening and formation of foci by the principle of unscheduled mnemonics. It also deals with the way in which translation into classificatory language differs from translation into a natural language. Incidentally it mentions some of the problems in library classification which await research.

The third chapter examines the social forces which have been shaping library classification — the force of democracy and of the social call for documentation created by the intensification of specialisation in the pursuit of knowledge. It emphasises that the unit for classification has changed from macroscopic masses embodied in books to microscopic units embodied in articles. It then refers to the pressure caused by the industries which have begun to build libraries of their own. Lastly it shows that a foundation which may prove sufficient to the classification of a closed system of knowledge will not be sufficient to handle a growing system.

The fourth chapter shows the limitations imposed on library classification by the fact that it seeks to transform a multi-dimensional continuum in the field of knowledge into a uni-directional uni-dimensional set of concrete objects — either books and kindred materials on the shelves or entries about them in the catalogue.

The fifth chapter shows the ways in which the library catalogue can make up for the limitations of library classification. It refers to the punched card system and the chain-procedure in the determination of class index entries as two effective modes of symbiosis between library classification and library catalogue.

The sixth chapter develops the concept of the capacity of library classification and deals with the effect of increase in the length of the base of notation and of the class numbers. It mentions the desirability of having a higher limit for the length of class numbers in documentation-work. It also shows the crowding of all the conjunctions or connecting symbols at a particular point in the ordinal scale of the basic symbols.

The seventh chapter shows how the dimensions of class numbers can be increased through optional facets without the unsightly accumulation of the debris of the conjunctions otherwise happening between vacant facets. It points out the lines along which research should proceed to make the classifier autonomous in determining the optional facets, their order and the foci in them.

The eighth chapter is devoted to the organisation necessary to make library classification evolve continuously to keep step with the formations in the field of knowledge. It stresses the need for a team of workers, indeed for the co-operation of five sub-teams. It also appeals to the Institute for Advanced Studies in Princeton, the Royal Society of London and similar bodies to provide for research in library classification, the IFLA and the F.I.D. to merge with each other and pursue this subject with undivided counsel and to the UNESCO to give the necessary aid to the amalgamated IFLA and F.I.D. to maintain a secretariate to develop library classification into a self-perpetuating international language of ordinal numbers capable of meeting with success any challenge from the field of knowledge.

S. R. RANGANATHAN.

University of Delhi,
February, 1949.

Chapter 1

EVOLUTION OF CLASSIFICATION

The function of classification and its connotation have been changing progressively.

101 In the Individual

Classification emerges very early as part of the mechanism of remembering and thinking. As soon as the number of concrete things to be seen, handled and possessed increases beyond a few in the field of interest of a child — this happens very early in childhood — the child instinctively begins to divide them into fairly homogeneous groups and to arrange the groups themselves in some helpful order. For example I have been observing during the last one year this natural tendency in the child of a neighbour of mine. I began to notice this tendency in the child when it was about twelve months old. I used to find it enjoying putting all the clothes together, all the toys together, all the books together and so on. Of late it is making sub-groups out of these. For example it separates its toys into those made of rubber, celluloid, wood, clay and so on. The celluloid articles are further divided into sub-groups like animal figures, human figures, balls, combs etc. This tendency to divide and group articles according to likeness of some sort persists throughout life. It is also extended from concrete materials to abstract ideas as one grows mentally. The degree to which the subdivision is carried out goes on increasing as the field of experience goes on deepening and widening. Ideas are analysed, grouped and thrown into a helpful sequence — that is classified — not only to facilitate memory but also to help thinking. In all these stages, classification may be said to be inexorable.

102 *In the Human Race*

The usual parallelism between ontogeny and phylogeny persists also in regard to mental characteristics. Humanity too, like individuals, had started classifying even in its very early infancy. *Vedic* literature, which is perhaps the oldest known specimen of the literary remains of the intellectual output of humanity, bristles everywhere with the effects of this human tendency to classify. Apart from evidence of systematic thinking and classified arrangement of thought, *Vedic* literature has sections devoted to the very process of classification — analysis, grouping and arrangement. The *Talmud* of the Babylonians and the hieroglyphics of the Egyptians confirm to an equal degree the early appearance of this tendency. The literary remains of the Greek civilisation of two thousand years ago cover classification as a discipline to such a remarkable degree that modern books on classification begin with Porphyry and Aristotle. Classification in a broad sense thus dates back from prehistoric times.

11 *The First Sense — Without Notation*

In those far off days, classification meant merely the mentioning of ideas or the arranging of materials in some systematic and helpful order. It did not mean anything more. A good deal of thought was no doubt spent on deciding which of the many possible permutations gave the most helpful order. There was even prolonged controversy on deciding this issue. The repetition of the controversy in regard to ideas and materials of different sorts led to the emergence of a science of classification. This led to a good deal of tidying up of concepts like likeness, difference, the qualities which an attribute should have to make it a useful basis or characteristic of classification and so on. Francis Bacon is a great name in this philosophy of classification. The practice of classification in vogue among those pursuing Natural Science added considerably to the literature on the subject. In due course classification became a distinctive subdivision of the discipline of logic — the logic of relation. This is classification in the first sense.

12 *The Second Sense — With Notation*

In its second sense, classification means what all is implied in its first sense and, in addition, the adoption of a mechanism by which the preferred order can be preserved and restored mechanically when disturbed. The term 'mechanically' is used to denote that the order is to be restored without going through the logic of relation *ab initio* but with the aid of a device which abstracts and visualises the order *qua* order, and is capable of being operated by one who has no notion of the relation which the arrangement seeks to respect and feature. This is the first major stage in the progress of the function and connotation of classification.

121 *Book-World*

It is those who had to care for books either as traders or as librarians that took this step forward and put more content into the concept of classification. Classification in the second ser e is being taken in the book-world through further stages of evolution. There is a reason why this has fallen to the share of those who handle books. In the case of those who handle other materials, they have to arrange the materials *qua* materials; and their shape, colour and other physical features themselves serve as the mechanism necessary to restore the old order. In the case of those who handle books, they have to arrange them not on the basis of their physical features but of their thought-content which is intangible to sensuous perception. The mechanism needed is, therefore, not inherent in the physical or mechanical properties of books. Something exotic has to be introduced. This takes the form of a mark or a symbol. It does not take long for this symbol to be an ordinal number. For after all, the ordinal number is by its very definition a symbol showing order.

122 *Library Classification*

It is this "piece of apparatus added to the classification" in the first sense which has led to classification in the second sense. The classification system of the Paris Booksellers which began to take shape in the seventeenth century and reached its fullest manifestation about the middle of the nineteenth century is the dominant example of a classification with a notation, elaborated by the book-world. Ismael Bouillaud and Jaques Charles Brunet were the first and the last names connected with the elaboration of this scheme.

Here is the sample of their scheme:

A	Theology
AI	Sacred writings
AI1	Text
AI1A	The whole Bible
AI1A*a*1 to AI1A*a*7	Polyglots
AI1A*m*80 to AI1A*m*83	Semitic languages
AI1A*m*80	Arabic
AI1A*m*81	Armenian
AI1A*m*82	Turkish
AI1A*n*84 to AI1A*n*99	Indian languages
AI1B	Old Testament
AI2	Interpretation
AII	Liturgy
B	Jurisprudence
C	Sciences and arts
D	Polite literature
E	History

Deciding on a particular order of arrangement for adoption and using a notation or a system of ordinal numbers as a means of mechanising the indication and preservation of the preferred order are two essential features of Library Classification.

13 Hospitality of Notation

The first widely influential classification which owed its origin to the library profession is the Decimal Classification. Its author was Melvil Dewey. It came out first in 1873 as a part of another book and in 1876 in the form of an independent book. It introduced a third feature in Library Classification. This feature concerned the notation. It may be described as Hospitality of Notation.

131 What

Hospitality depends upon and denotes a notational device which admits of interpolation and extrapolation of new ordinal numbers amidst and outside the already existing sequence. In the notation of the Bibliothèque Nationale fitted to the system of Paris Booksellers, this is not possible. For example, consider the number AI1A*m*82 given in section 122. Here if a new subsection crops up between AI1A*m* and AI1A*n*, the notation is unable to receive it in its appropriate place. Similarly if a new section crops up between AI1A and AI1B, the notation is unable to receive it in its appropriate place. Similar remarks apply to the cropping up of new subdivisions, new divisions and new main classes — these are classificatory terms, by the way, occuring in the passage of Berwick Sayers quoted in section 122.

A system of notation that does not admit of interpolation and extrapolation may be said to be inhospitable or rigid. One that admits of it may be said to be hospitable or elastic. Hospitality may also be described as Expansibility. This term was used by Charles Ammi Cutter in the name of his classification *viz.* Expansive Classification which was brought out in 1891.

132 How

The device employed in the Decimal Classification to secure hospitality of notation is the fixing of the place-values of the digits of a number as if it were a pure decimal fraction. Thus

336 (= Public Finance) lies between 33 (= Economics) and 34 (= Law);
3362 (= Taxation) lies between 336 (= Public Finance) and 337 (= Tariff);
33621 (= Direct Taxes) lies between 3362 (= Taxation) and 3363 (= Public Debt); an so on.

The correct sequence of the ordinal numbers given above is

33; 336; 3362; 33621; 3363; 337; 34

as these are to be read as pure decimal fractions.

But if they were read as pure integers the sequence would have been 33; 34; 336; 337; 3362; 3363; 33621

If such integral notation were used, Public Finance which is a subdivision or subordinate class of Economics cannot be accommodated between 33 Economics and 34 Law; nor can taxation be placed between 336 Public Finance and 337 Tariff; and so on. The decimal-fraction-notation, on the other hand, enables us to interpolate Public Finance between Economics and Law and thus bring it close to its parent class Economics; and so also with the other subclasses. As illustrated above, there is no limit to the chain of successively subordinated classes which can be interpolated if the decimal-fraction-notation is used.

The most potent and lasting contribution of the Decimal Classification to the philosophy of library classification is the demonstration of the practicability of securing Hospitality of Notation by the simple device of Decimal Fraction Notation. This is a third feature which any scheme of library classification is now expected to have.

14 *Hospitality at Many Points*

The Colon Classification is another scheme of classification contributed by the library profession. It came out first in 1933. It adopted the decimal-fraction-notation and went a step further. For it introduced a fourth feature in library classification. This feature too concerned the notation. It may be described as Hospitality or Expansibility at Many Points.

141 *What*

The following concrete cases will elucidate the concept of "Hospitality at Many Points". The subjects are fitted with Decimal Notation. Consider

616	Disease
616.3	Disease of the digestive system
616.33	Disease of the stomach
616.334	Diseases of the pylorus

We can thus continue the subdivision on the basis of the organ as far as we like. Hospitality of Notation resides, as it were, at the right end of the notation. In other words, it is expansible at the right end.

But the subject may also be subdivided on the basis of the nature of disease like Infectious Disease, Tuberculosis and so on of the Digestive system, or the Stomach or the Pylorus as the case may be. It is the second 6 in the notation that stands for Disease. Its right side is blocked by the number which stands for the organ which is diseased. It is not therefore possible to add further digits after that 6 so as to represent subdivisions of disease like Infectious Disease and Tuberculosis. To put it in other words, Hospitality in Notation is not possible at the point were there is a change-over from Problem to Organ. It is not expansible at such a point. To put it in general terms, no Hospitality in Notation can reside at the junction of two trains of characteristics of division — say, in this case, the train of Problem characteristics and that of Organ characteristics. It can reside only at the end of the last train of characteristics. This is a serious limitation in the Hospitality of Notation. It is desirable to eliminate this limitation and make the notation expansible wherever the part of the notation pertaining to any train of characteristics ends — and not merely the last train.

The following Colon Notation for the various subjects considered above eliminates the limitation and provides for Hospitality of Notation at the junctions of trains of characteristics also. It must be remembered that, in the Colon Classification, the Organ Characteristic comes first and the Problem characteristic second.

L2:4	Disease of the digestive system
L2:42	Infectious disease of the digestive system
L2:421	Tuberculosis of the digestive system

So far it is only the Hospitality residing at the end of the notation that is demonstrated. In other words it shows only that the end of the problem-part of the notation is expansible. Next consider:

L2:4	Disease of the digestive system
L24:4	Disease of stomach

L246:4	Disease of the glands of the stomach
L2463:4	Disease of the pylora

Here Hospitality of Notation is seen to reside also to the left of the symbol ":" which really marks the change-over from the train of Organ characteristics to that of Problem characteristics. In other words, this set of the subjects shows that the organ part of the notation which is not the last part, is equally expansible.

The following shows that we can simultaneously invoke the Hospitality of Notation residing at the end of the notation as well as at the junctions between trains of characteristics. In other words, we can simultaneously expand the Organ part as well as the Problem part of the notation.

L2:4	Disease of the digestive system
L24:42	Infectious disease of stomach
L246:421	Tuberculosis of the glands of the stomach
L2463:421	Tuberculosis of pylora.

If we introduce a third train of characteristics, the Hospitality of Notation will reside in a third point of the notation also and it can be invoked simultaneously at all the three points. Here is a demonstration: —

L2:4:6	Treatment for disease of digestive system
L24:42:62	Physical treatment for infectious disease of stomach
L246:421:625	Radiotheraphy for tuberculosis of the stomach glands
L2463:421:6252	Ultra-violet theraphy for tuberculosis of pylora

This can be generalised. The Hospitality of Notation resides not only at the end but also at each of the junctions between trains of characteristics. It resides, in fact, in as many points as there are trains of characteristics. It is a case of Hospitality or Expansibility at Many Points.

142 How

How does the Colon Classification provide for Hospitality at Many Points? Apparently it is through the use of the symbol ":". The ordinal value of this symbol is defined in the scheme by the statement that it lies between 0 and 1. It is this which place the trick so to speak. The name Colon Classification was given to the scheme on account of the great potency which the symbol colon has secured in the provision of hospitality. But to say that the Hospitality at Many Points is due to the symbol colon is to miss the essence of the matter. Any other symbol might have been used to produce the same result.

1421 Facet-Analysis

The essential feature of the Colon Classification which has led to Hospitality or Expansibility at Many Points is what has been termed Facet-Analysis in the *Library classification: Fundamentals and procedure* (1944). Facet-analysis is the mental process by which the possible trains of characteristics which can form the basis of classification of a subject are enumerated and the exact measure in which the attributes concerned are incident in the subject are determined.

Facets are inherent in the subject. They should therefore characterise the notation also. They stand visualised in the structure of the Colon Notation. The parts of this notation corresponding to the different facets of the subject stand apart and they are linked up by a connecting symbol. For example, when the problem is disease the Main Subject Medicine admits of the Facet-formula:

L [O] : [P] : [H]

Medicine [Organ] : [Problem] : [Handling]

The Facet-Structure of the Specific Subject:

Ultra-violet therapy for tuberculosis of pylora is:

Medicine [of Pylora] : [for tuberculosis] : [Ultra-violet therapy]

The notation for this is:

L2463:421:6252

The correspondance between the facets of the subject and those of the notation is obvious. The facet-structure of the notation is thrown into unmistakeable relief by the occurrence of the connecting symbol.

One of the most potent and lasting contributions of the Colon Classification to the philosophy of library classification is the demonstration of the practicability of securing Hospitality or Expansibility at Many Points of Notation by Facet-Analysis and its reflection in the notation by the use of a distinctive symbol with specified ordinal value to connect the facets in the Notation. This is a fourth feature which has appeared in library classification and which future schemes of classification may possibly incorporate with profit.

15 Hospitality of a Second Kind

The kind of hospitality which was discussed in sections 13 and 14 is turned on a chain of subordinate classes of successive removes or orders of intension — something like providing a chain of houses for persons of successive generations like the son, the grandson, the great grandson etc. in a filiatory order. There is also another kind of hospitality like that of providing an array of houses for the successive brothers of one and the same generation in the order of age or seniority. The second kind of hospitality is turned on an array of co-ordinate classes of the same remove or order of intension. Hospitality of this kind too demands a notational device for its being implemented.

151 Decimal Classification

In the Decimal Classification, the base of the notation consists of the ten arabic Numerals, 0, 1, 2 ...... 9. The field of knowledge is, therefore, divided in the first instance, into ten co-ordinate Main Classes *i. e.* classes of the first order of intension or of the first order, in brief. At the further stages of division, the digit 0 is reserved for indicating divisions based on the form of exposition of the whole class and only the smaller base consisting of the remaining nine digits is available to represent co-ordinate subclasses of a substantial nature. Thus only nine co-ordinate subclasses can be accomodated by the notation at any of the further stages of division. One way in which this limitation is overcome is to make the digits 1, 2....8 represent eight co-ordinate subclasses and make the digit 9 represent collectively all the remaning co-ordinate subclasses. While this device makes the division totally exhaustive, it fails to make it mutually exclusive. Occassionally, the ninth subclass is represented by 91 instead of by 9, the tenth sub-class by 92 and so on with freedom to accommodate sixteen subclasses, the sixteenth being represented by 98 and the number 99 made to represent collectively all the remaining subclasses.

152 Colon Classification

In the Colon Classification, the last-mentioned device is used not occasionally but as a rule and it is further generalised. The seventeenth subclass is represented by 991, the eighteenth by 992 and so on up to the twenty-fourth being represented by 998, and again the twenty-fifth subclass is represented by 9991, the twenty-seventh by 9992 and so on up to the thirty-second being represented by 9998; this device can be repeated *ad infinitum.* Thus it is not merely 8, nor merely 16, not even merely 24, but an endless number of co-ordinate subclasses which can be numbered.

153 Octave Notation

This principle has been called Octave Principle; the notation may be called Octave Notation; and the digit 9 which ceases to represent anything in particular may be called Octavising Digit. The surrender of one of the nine digits — giving it up without using it to represent a division — has produced the capacity to represent an infinity of divisions. This is in conformity with the saying in the *Bhagavadgita* that sacrifice begets plenty and with the parallel sayings in the Holy Bible and the sacred books of every other religion.

154 Hospitality in Array

The Hospitality provided by the Octave Notation has been called Hospitality in Array in the *Prolegomena to library classification* (1937). In contradistinction, the hospitality provided by the Decimal-Fraction-Notation has been called Hospitality in Chain.

155 F.I.D. and Octave Notation

The Octave Notation is one of the contributions of the Colon Classification to the philosophy of classification. This is a fifth feature of library classification. It was officially adopted by the International Federation for Documentation in its Conference at the Hague in June 1948. To get the benefits of this notation fully and comfortably, it is necessary for a scheme of library classification to conform to the Canon of Unscheduled Mnemonics enunciated in the *Prolegomena* and described also in section 26 of chapter 2 of this book.

16 Multiplicity of Main Classes: Compound Specific Subjects

Consider subjects like the following:

Group 1 (Bias-Relation)

Colon Number		Universal Decimal Number
BOD	Mathematics for engineers	51:62
B280X81	Statistics for actuaries	31:519.5
B334:1:2:10D66:2	Numerical integration of linear partial differential equations of second order for designers of electrical transmission lines.	517.946.5:621.319[1]

Group 2 (Tool-Relation)

Colon Number		Universal Decimal Number
X:B	Mathematical study of economic problems	33:51
X81:B28	Actuarial science	519.5
T4:475:P:7:7:B28	Statistical study of the marking of composition papers in university examinations.	371.26:428.2:31[2]

[1] The U.D.C. number of the third example fails to represent the focus in the Problem Facet *viz.* Numerical Integration.

[2] The U.D.C. number of the third example fails to represent the focus in the Educand Facet *viz.* University.

Group 3 (Influence-Relation)

Colon Number		Universal Decimal Number
W.*k*U	Geopolitics	32:91
X72.*k*R4	Taxation and ethics	336.2:17
L2:3.*k*S:524	Digestion of angry persons	612.3:179.8

In each of the nine subjects mentioned above, two main classes or specific subjects belonging to two main classes are involved. They are brought into relation with one another. In the first group, the relation is one of bias. One of the two subjects forms the subject of exposition and the other subject merely determines the angle from which it is expounded. The result is a specific subject involving bias-relation. In the second group, the relation is one of tool. One of the two subjects forms the subject of exposition and the other subject is used merely as a tool for investigation. The result is a specific subject involving tool-relation. In the third group, the relation is one of influence. One of the two subjects forms the subject of exposition and it is the influence by the other subject that is expounded. The result is a specific subject involving influence-relation. There are other known kinds of relation *e. g.* aspect and comparison. Still other kinds of relation may be involved.

In library classification, new Compound Specific Subjects are deemed to get created by such relations between two subjects. Such a new compound specific subject has to be represented by a notation of its own. It will be a convenience if its notation is tell-tale in the sense that it readily discloses the constituent subjects, their respective notations and the kind of relation involved.

161 Decimal Classification

In the Decimal Classification, the notation of such a compound specific subject has the first two of these desirable qualities. With regard to the third, the connecting symbol 0005 is used to denote comparison-relation and 0001 is used to denote every other kind of relation. The latter leads to a mixing up of different compound specific subjects. That is, classification fails.

162 The Universal Decimal Classification

In the Universal Decimal Classification ":" is the only symbol to show relation of any kind. Thus, the third desirable quality is absent in the notation of compound specific subjects. This leads to homonyms, which a classificatory language is expected to avoid.

163 The Colon Classification

In the Colon Classification, an attempt is made to distinguish compound specific subjects involving different kinds of relation. The different kinds of relation are distinguished by the use of different connecting symbols. For example,

0 is used to denote bias relation; and

: and in certain specified circumstances :9 are used to denote tool and aspect relations.

The fourth edition, which is under preparation, seeks to distinguish other kinds of relation. It may be as follows:

:*h* to denote comparison
:*k* to denote 'influenced by'
:*m* to denote 'stimulated by'
:*n* to denote 'suppressed by'
:*s* to denote 'influencing'
:*t* to denote 'stimulating'
:*u* to denote 'suppressing'

164 Phase-Analysis

In *Library classification: Fundamentals and procedure,* such a compound specific subject is said to be multi-phased. The breaking of it into its components is called Phase-Analysis. The component which is the subject of exposition is called the Primary Phase. The second component which is brought into a subordinate relation with it is called the Secondary Phase. If there be a third component, it is called a Tertiary Phase. A fourth component, if it exists, is called a Quaternary Phase and so on. The second and the later phases may be of any kind.

Here is an example of a four-phased compound specific subject:

Franchini (A.). Suicide in Genoa: statistical and medicc legal contributions

Here is the result of phase-analysis:

Primary phase	*Secondary phase*	*Tertiary phase*	*Quaternary phase*
Suicide in Genoa	Statistical	medico	legal contributions

Here is the Colon Notation for the above:

Y1:4511:2:53CG:9B280L0Z

The Primary Phase shows four facets according to the facet formula

Y1 [Gr] : [P] : [S] : [G]

Sociology [Group] : [Problem] : [Secondary Problem] : [Geographical]

The Secondary phase is a tool-phase, while the tertiary and the quaternary phases are both bias-phases

One of the contributions to the philosophy of library classification, which was initiated by the Decimal Classification in a small way, emphasised by the Universal Decimal Classification and being elaborated to a greater degree by the Colon Classification, is Phase-Analysis. This is a sixth feature which has appeared in library classification. This is a feature which all future schemes of classification may perhaps retain with advantage.

171 Evolution and Schemes of Library Classification

The Congress Classification has carried the enumeration of classes in a helpful order to a remarkable degree. But it has neglected to develop the notation in a progressive and expressive manner. It has thus stepped out of the dominant line of evolution of library classification. Its method of providing for only limited hospitality by leaving gaps amidst integers is primitive; and even this gap is to be shared promiscuously by hospitality in chain and hospitality in array. Its still-born notation is dead and insensitive to facet-analysis and phase-analysis. The liberal size of the gaps amidst integers is postponing notational crash. But they cannot hold forth long against the mounting onslaughts of the new formations in the field of knowledge.

172 *Expansive and Subject Classification*

The Expansive and Subject Classifications mark stages of exploration and experiment in Hospitality of Notation and Analysis of Facets and Phases. They showed the direction which evolution may follow with profit. But they did not have the structural make-up to persist in that direction.

173 *The Decimal and the Universal Decimal Classification*

It is the Decimal and the Universal Decimal Classifications that lay in the true line of evolution. They represent the successive landmarks of importance. The U.D.C. would have carried the evolution further if it had not attached itself so rigidly to the D.C. as its core. The D.C. has clipped its wings and acted as a drag. It has totally denied the adoption of facet-analysis and has rendered phase-analysis quite feeble.

174 *The Colon Classification*

The Colon Classification has taken the evolution to a further stage by a conscious embellishment of facet- and phase-analysis. Even this makes it represent another landmark of importance. The next chapter will examine a still further stage of evolution to which it is taking library classification.

Chapter 2

LIBRARY CLASSIFICATION — AN ARTIFICIAL LANGUAGE

Perhaps it is right to say that the latest major stage in the evolution of library classification is expressed in the view that a system of Class Numbers constructed according to a scheme of classification constitute an Artificial Language of Ordinal Numbers — a Classificatory Language in short . Classification is the process of translation of the name of a specific subject from a natural language to a classificatory language. Class Number is the translation. Classifier is the translator. Classificationist is the designer of the classificatory language.

21 *Specification*

The qualities which the designer seeks to secure for a classificatory language are given below with illustrations taken from the Colon, Decimal or Universal Decimal Classifications:—

211 *Ordinal Value*

11 Each basic symbol or character or digit, as it may be called, has a definite ordinal value in relation to the others;

12 Each class number has a definite ordinal value in relation to the others;

13 The ordinal value of a class number is derived uniquely from the ordinal values of its component digits in accordance with prescribed rules.

212 *Phonemes*

21 Whereas in a natural language each character has only a phonetic value but no semantic value and represents only a phoneme, in a

classificatory language each basic symbol or digit or character has a semantic value and represents one or more fundamental ideas;

Examples

Natural language: N is Phoneme; it has no semantic value or meaning.

Colon language: N means Fine Arts or Twentieth Century
3 means Cyclopaedia, or Analysis, or Physiology etc.

Decimal language: 6 means Society or Establishment or Africa etc.

22 Whereas in a natural language the sequential or ordinal value traditionally assigned to the characters is ignored (Except in a dictionary) in arranging sentences formed of them, in classificatory language the ordinal value assigned to the characters is, as a rule, invoked at all times in arranging any class numbers whatever, formed of them,

Examples

Natural language: The sentences "I went to him. He was there. All was right" are not arranged alphabetically *i.e.* according to the traditional ordinal values of the characters A.B.C. etc., but according to the sequence of thought.

Colon language: The class numbers B3, C5, E7 etc., whatever be their number, are always arranged according to their ordinal values which are themselves derived from the ordinal values of the digits 1,2 . . . . . 9, A,B,E, etc.

Decimal language: The class numbers 34, 52, 63 etc. whatever be their number, are always arranged according to this ordinal values which are themselves derived from the ordinal values of the digits 0, 1, 2 etc.

23 Whereas the fixing of the ordinal and phonetic values of the characters of a natural language had happened in prehistoric times and the semantic values of the words are always subject to slow

changes inherent in their use by a mass of people over whom there can be no possible inexorable sanction to enforce eternal conformity, the ordinal and semantic values of the characters of a classificatory language are fixed by the classificationist who may be an expert individual or a small expert body, and are rigidly enforced at all times on all who use them, the right to change any of them being reserved solely in the expert.

Examples

Natural language: Take the word 'library' itself. It originally meant a place for writing books, then a place for housing books, then an institution charged with the care of books, then an institution where books are kept and produced for use on demand and now it means an institution wher·· reading and kindred materials are kept and which is charged with the duty of inviting people to use them for relaxation, information, and inspiration or all leading to the perpetual furtherance of self-education.

Colon language: N has been assigned two possible meanings and the context in which each meaning has to be used; it is not open to any one but the person or body in charge of the designing of the language to alter its meaning.

Decimal language: 33 has been assigned the meaning Economics; it is not open to any one but the person or body in charge of the designing of the language to alter its meaning.

213 *The Elements*

31 A classificatory language has only substantives and conjunctions.[1]

32 Syntactical relation is shown in it entirely by position without any dependence on morphological changes or prepositions; and

33 It is a pure agglutinative language

Examples

Natural language: In the phrase "Statistical study of the growth of living organisms", the substantives "Statistical study", "Growth" and "Living organism" are brought together. The mere juxtaposition of the first two words may mean either "Statistical study of growth" or "Growth of statistical study". It is their disposition with reference to the preposition "of" which determines what is meant. Sometimes morphological variation as in "Rama's book" does the same work. Sometimes position alone does the work as in "Rama saw Krishna".

Colon language: In G:7:B28 which stands for "Statistical study of the growth of living organism", G,7,B,2 and 8 are substantives and the colons are conjunctions. They are assembled without any morphological changes or the aid of prepostions. The different

[1] This is rendered possible because

(1) it has to translate only *names* of specific subjects;

(2) adjectives qualifying nouns in the natural language can either be thrown into the form of a noun or be reckoned as an inseparable part of the name,

Example

In a classificatory language "Indian History" is thrown in the form of "India. History". But in "Digestive system", the adjective is deemed inseparable from the noun it qualifies;

(3) it will have no occasion to translate verbs and their adverbs and other auxiliaries.

meanings are got by changing their relative position and nothing else.

Decimal language: In 574.1340001311 which also means the same thing, 0001 is a conjunction and each of the other digits is a substantive. They are assembled without any morpohological changes or the aid of prepositions. The Colon Classification uses 0, :, . and - as conjunctions. The Universal Decimal Classification uses :, /, 0, () etc. as conjunctions.

214 Semantics

41 In a classificatory language, there is a strict one-one correspondence between class numbers and names of specific subjects,

i.e. the name of each specific subject can be translated into one and only one class number and each class number can denote one and only one specific subject,

i.e. there is no synonym or homonym:

42 There is a one-many correspondence between the basic digits of the classificatory language and the fundamental ideas which they can denote,

i.e. any fundamental idea will always be represented by the same basic digit, although a basic digit may be used to represent many fundamental ideas;

43 The interpretation of a class number, and for this purpose of each of its component digits, is on the Gestalt basis,

i.e. the meaning of a digit in a class number is determined by the entire set of digits along with which it stands combined and by the position it occupies in the whole pattern of the class number;

Examples

Colon language: In the Gestalt L4:4:4,
the first 4 = Respiratory system;
the second 4 = Disease; and
the third 4 = Pathology

In the Gestalt Z44:4,

the first 4 = Asia
the second 4 = India
the third 4 = Torts

44 The Gestalt value of a digit in a class number is fixed as rigidly as its ordinal value,

i.e. its meaning is both unique and unchanging,

i.e. its meaning is not subject to fluctuation in the way in which the meaning of a word in a natural language is subject to fluctuation.

This is because the natural language evolves or drifts in the mouths of the masses whereas the classificatory language is an artificial one which is not exposed to the influence of the masses and is strictly controlled and maintained by a small body of experts.

215 Representation

51 A class number is easy to write;

52 It admits of speed of writing;

53 It is generally brief, subject to the Canon of Relativity,

i.e. the number of digits in a class number may increase with the degree or order of intension of the specific subject it represents.

Examples

"Mathematics" which is a broad subject is represented by the single digit B in Colon Classification and by the two digits 51 in Universal Decimal Classification;

"Mathematical analysis" which is of greater intension is represented by the two digits B3 in C.C. and by the three digits 517 in U.D.C.

"Numerical integration of linear partial differential equations of second order for designers of electrical transmission lines" which is of very great intension is represented in Colon Classification by B334:1:2:10D66:2 which has 16 digits; and in Universal Decimal Classification by 517.946.5:621.319 which has 17 digits. The remark on the latter number given in section 16 should be remembered *viz.* the focus 'Numerical integration' is unrepresented.

216 Basic Purpose

61 When arranged by their class numbers, the specific subjects fall in the preferred helpful order.

62 When new specific subjects are born, they can be given class numbers which drop them in the preferred helpful place amidst those which exist already.

63 The above two purposes are fulfilled whether a specific subject is

(1) a bare main class of the scheme; or

(2) a simple subclass of the first order formed by *dissecting* the main class *i.e.* by sharpening the focus; or

(3) a simple subclass of high order formed by denuding it *i.e.* by sharpening the focus to a higher degree; or

(4) a composite subclass formed by *laminating* foci of any degree of sharpness belonging to two or more of the *facets* inherent to the main class *i.e.* by the formation of a *composite* focus; or

(5) a compound subclass formed by the *loose* assembling of specific subjects formed by any or all of the above means from two or more main classes *i.e.* by the assembling of two or more *phases i.e.* by the formation of a *compound* focus; or

(6) a formal subclass formed by *dressing* the focus got by any or all of the above means in a particular form of exposition, single or superimposed *i.e.* by the formation of a *dressed* focus.

The ideas and the terminology used above were first introduced in the memoir on *Classification and international documentation* published as V.14 F.4 of the *Review of documentation* of the F.I.D. (International Federation for Documentation). Illustrations with graphical representation will be found in that memoir. Some examples have also occurred in chap. 1 of this book.

22 The Schedules

The schedules of a scheme of classification constitute the *dictionary* of the classificatory language formed by it. They arrange the elements of that language in accordance with their ordinal values quite in keeping with the genius of that language and give against each element its meaning in a natural language. The dictionary needed to work in the opposite direction is the *index* to the schedules. It arranges the elements of a natural language alphabetically and gives against each element its meaning in the classificatory language.

221 *Tourist Conversation Book* *Congress Classification*

The schedules of the Congress Classification typify the schedules of most of the classificatory languages designed till now. They are like a Tourist Conversation Book rather than a Dictionary. The former lists not only fundamental words but also their declensional forms, and phrases, clauses and sentences formed by combining one or more of them. So also the schedules of the Congress Classification give *ready-made* class numbers of all specific subjects believed to exist or anticipated to come into existence. When new specific subjects — not anticipated and listed by the classificationist — appear, the schedules fail the classifier. He can not coin class numbers to represent the new subjects. The classificationist alone can coin them in every case. They are coined in such an arbitrary way that the linguistic nature of the Congress Class Number System is suppressed from one's thought.

222 *Tourist Conversation Book plus* *Decimal Classification*

The schedules of the Decimal Classification show a slight tendency to step off from the status of a pure tourist conversation book. The supplementary tables — 3 Languages and Literatures and 4 Philological Divisions — make a beginning in introducing a dash of dictionary element in two of the Main Classes. In these tables the system of ready-made class numbers of composite specific subjects being given by the classificationist is abandoned in favour of giving the classifier freedom to construct their class numbers from schedules which list only the component terms of which their names are composed. For example, the Decimal Classification does not give the class numbers shown against the following subjects in a ready-made form:

Inflection of Russian adjectives	491.7516
Orthography of Chinese vowels	495.12
Malayalam prose composition	894.81282
Prakrit Slang	831.31709
Russian romantic poetry	891.7103
Chinese Drama	895.2
Malayalam fiction	894.8123
Prakrit prose	891.314

The classifier has to construct them taking the constituent numbers — strictly speaking — from four schedules:

From 'First Summary', he should take

4	Philology
8	Literature

From 'Supplementary table 3', he should take

9131	Prakrit
917	Russian
94812	Malayalam
95	Chinese

From 'Supplementary table 4', he should take

12	Orthography of vowels
516	Inflection of adjectives
709	Slang
82	Composition of prose

From the table for '8 Literature', he should take

103	Romantic Poetry
2	Drama
3	Fiction
4	Prose

These component parts should be assembled according to prescribed rules. This is similar to what is done while translating from one language to another: the sentence in the first language is analysed and the units are re-arranged in accordance with the syntactical requirements of the second language. Each unit is translated with the aid of the dictionary — which lists only the units and not sentences. The translations of the units are assembled so as to form a sentence of the second language.

Supplementary table '2 Uniform Subdivisions' goes the whole hog in this direction and lists "0 Form divisions", "00 Viewpoints" and "000 Miscellaneous common subdivisions" which are combinable with any class occurring in the "Complete Tables". This amounts to a recognition that the Dictionary-concept is more potent than the Concept of Tourist Conversation Book as an aid to translation from one language to another.

Moreover there are pockets of the dictionary element found scattered through the Complete Tables. See for example notes like the following:

016	Bibliography of special subjects *Subdivided like the main classification from 000—999.*
338.45	Machinery in industry *May be divided like 620—699 with .4561 divided like the whole classification for other industries*
581.2323	Algal diseases *Divided like 589.3.-.6*

223 More of Dictionary Feature
Universal Decimal Classification

The preliminary elaboration of auxiliary tables by the Universal Decimal Classification invests its schedules with more of the dictionary feature. The auxiliary tables concern themselves really with the listing of component ideas which can be combined to yield specific subjects, even as a dictionary lists component words which can be combined to yield sentences. Here is an extract from the section entitled 'Outline structure of the classification'. "Auxiliary classes are separate sets representing notions such as are commonly employed to pecify subjects more minutely. There are thus provided in the Universal Decimal Classification five sets of Auxiliary Tables of Common Subdivision of Language, Form, Place, Time, Point of View". Provision is also made for combination of Main Classes as and when required. Further there is a scheme of Analytical Subdivisions scattered throughout the schedules in the form of notes at the head of several classes in addition to the pockets of dictionary element scattered throughout the core of the Decimal Classification which the Universal Decimal Classification has adopted.

224 *Expansive and Subject Classifications*

The evolution of the idea of replacing the tourist-conversation-book-type of schedules by the dictionary-type began very early with the Expansive Classification. Its auxiliary tables represent the emergence of the dictionary type in an incipient form. The Categorical Tables of the Subject Classification carried the evolution into a blind lane as it were. This arrested further evolution.

225 *Dictionary and Grammar*
Colon Classification

The view that a system of class numbers constitute a language — an artificial language of ordinal numbers — had yet to be taken along more productive lines of evolution. A full manifestation of such a view would demand the linguistics of a classificatory language being developed like the linguistics of any natural language. It should be provided with its own analogues of Orthography, Morphology, Syntax, Semasiology and Rules of Composition, Interpretation and Translation. These elements took a more recognisable shape for the first time in the Colon Classification. The wording of Rule 02 of chapter 0 of part 1 of the *Colon classification*

"A Class Number is a symbolic translation (of the name) of the subject of the book"

may perhaps be taken to indicate that there was a feeling at the subconscious level that a regular classificatory linguistics had become necessary to meet the demands on library classification by the incessant new formations in the field of knowledge and their repercussion on the efficiency of reference service — particularly that specialised form of it which has later come to be called Documentation Service. While teaching Decimal and Colon Classifications on a comparative basis to the students of Library Science, the concept of classificatory language slowly established itself and it came to the conscious level when the experience of teaching the subject came to be recorded in 1944 in the *Library Classification: Fundamentals and procedure.* The first part of this book is totally turned on this concept. The first two chapters of the second part are devoted to the laying down of a systematic procedure for translation from natural to classificatory language and vice versa. All the examples in classification are worked out as exercises in translation.

In the *Colon classification* itself, the schedules are out and out of the dictionary variety. Except in the illustrative schedules of classics, there is no vestige of the tourist conversation book. The dictionary feature not only gets emphasised in the preliminary schedules of Main Classes, Common subdivisions, Geographical Divisions, Language Divisions and Chronological Divisions, but also pervades one and all of the chapters giving the detailed schedules of the several main classes. Each of these chapters gives, not ready-made class numbers as in the Decimal or the Universal Decimal Classification, but the schedules for each of the facets of the main class treated. The divisions enumerated in these schedules are not by themselves specific subjects. This corresponds to the elements (words) in a dictionary not being sentences.

Examples

(1) Chapter S Psychology of part 2 of the *Colon classification* gives two schedules: The first for the Entity or the kind of person whose pshychology is studied and the second for the Problem studied. The first schedule gives divisions like

1 Child; 2 Adolescent; 25 Adolescent girl and so on.

The second gives divisions like

2 Sensation; 5 Emotion; 56 Anxiety and so on.

To translate the name of the specific subject "Psychological study of anxiety in adolescent girls", we first throw the terms of the name of the specific subject in the order demanded by the syntax of the classificatory language. This is prescribed by the rules of chapter

S Psychology of part 1 of the *Colon classification* and is also summarised at the heading of chapter S Psychology of part 2 in the form of the facet formula: —

S [E] : [P]

which means

Psychology [Entity] : [Problem]

Following this formula, we rearrange the words in the name of the specific subject as follows:

Psychological study [in adolescent girls] : [of anxiety]

We next translate the focus in each facet with the aid of the schedules already referred to. We get

S25:56

(2) Chapter X Economics of part 2 gives the schedule of the divisions or the foci in the two facets "Business" and "Economic Problem" of Economics. The facet-formula at the head of the chapter indicates two more facets *viz.* "Geographical" and "Chronological", the schedules of whose foci are given in the preliminary chapters 3 and 5 of part 2. The schedule for the Business Facet mentions foci like

4 Transport; 7L Banking; 9 Industry; 9J Agricultural Industry; 9J771 Agricultural Industry of Cotton Crop and so on.

The schedule for the Economic Problem Facet mentions foci like

2 Production; 51 Marketing; 6 Financing; 7 Value; 75 Planned Economy and so on.

The schedule of geographical divisions in chapter 3 mentions foci like

5 Europe; 7 America; 73 United States and so on.

The schedule of Chronological Divisions in chapter 5 mentions foci like

N 1900 — 1999

and the rules in chapter 5 of part 1 show that 1930 is to be translated as N3. To translate the name of the specific subject "Government control of cotton production in the United States during the 1930's", we first throw these words in the order demanded by the syntax of the classificatory language as symbolised by the Facet-Formula at the head of chapter X Economics of part 2. We get successively: —

X [B] : [G] : [C]

Economics [Business] : [Economic Problem] : [Geographical Division] : [Chronological Division]

Economics [of cotton production] : [of Government Control] : [in the United States] : [during the 1930's]

X9J771:75:73:N3

(3) Consider the translation of the name of the specific subject: — *Quantitative-anatomical analysis of the leaves of the rice plants grown under different conditions* by O. M. Radkevich.

When rearranged as demanded by the syntax of the classificatory language we get, on supplying the ellipses 'Agriculture' and 'Biology' and dropping the puff 'under different conditions': —

Agriculture [Food] [Seeds] [Rice] : [Biology] [Leaves] : [Anatomical] : [Quantitative analysis]

We pick up the translation of the different elements of the above from different chapters of part 2 as follows:

Element No.	Chapter and schedule which give the translation	
1	1	Main Class
2	J	Agriculture. Schedule U Utility
3	J	Agriculture. Schedule P Part
4	J	Agriculture. Schedule C Crop
5	1	Main Class
6	I	Botany. Schedule O Organ
7	G	Biology. Schedule P Problem
8	B	Mathematics

The final translation turns out to be

J381:G5:2:B28

These examples demonstrate how effectively the evolution of library classification is reaching the stage of translation — with the aid of a dictionary and the rules of grammar -- from a natural language into an artificial language of ordinal numbers, that is a classificatory language, that is a scheme of classification.

23 *On Translation*

Like all others a classificatory language is necessarily conventional and cannot be used without a knowledge of the conventions it obeys. But translation into it differs in some respects from those into natural languages.

231 *Literary Translation*

In the process of literary translation a continual, subtle interchange takes place between two equally plastic elements, till their differences are resolved in a final adjustment. Since both parties to the intercourse (both languages) are, so to speak, living personalities, only a living personality can result: it is an unpredictable child that embodies imponderables from either side and can itself be judged only as a unique personality. And the same partners may produce other children, each perfect in its own way as an expression of their union by bringing out, now more, now less, of this or that capacity or characteristic of his parents — the same text, if it is at all highly organised, may be 'perfectly' translated in different ways. Perfection here is not scientific because both terms are almost indefinitely variable.

232 *Classificatory Translation*

But a classificatory language is invariable and translation into it is, therefore, a steady one-way process which can have only one conventionally perfect result. Not only is the result formally predetermined, but the process also is governed by the fact that one pole is fixed; the whole operation is canalised in the translator's mind by his knowledge of the fixed form in the classificatory language, which therefore operates like a magnetic field.

The effect of the scheme of classification in the determination of the specific subject may be visualised in another way. "A thin plate of metal .... is mounted in a horizontal position .... A small amount of sand is sprinkled over the plate, and a violin bow is used to set the plate singing .. The sand dances about and is soon thrown from vibrating parts of the plate and collects at the nodal lines." A beautiful pattern — Chladni's figures — is formed (see pictures of

Pp. 174 and 176 of *Sound* by Arthus Taber Jones, 1937). The pattern is determined by the vibrating qualities peculiar to the plate. So also the Phase- and Facet-Analysis peculiar to the classificatory language will throw the name of the specific subject of a book into a distinct form, peculiar to the classificatory language.

For the classifier in whom Phase- and Facet-Analysis have become second nature, classification is an almost automatic process: his thought is guided from the start by the preferred scheme of classification.

233 *Canalisation*

A critical examination of the language of the title and of the contents of the books is a necessary precaution against ambiguity, vagueness and rhetoric. The classifier must be prepared to fill up ellipses. This examination should follow the route prescribed by the needs of the preferred classificatory language. In dealing with connotation — the adherent as distinguished from the inherent signification — the translator has a delicate task before him. He must have a keen eye for specific details. His purpose should be to bring out the dominant specific subject (Primary Phase) in full and the adjectival ones (Secondary and other Phases) in a due subordination and in proper sequence so as to expose the heart of the author's intention and achievement. The classifier should suppress his own personal views (Canon of Reticence: *Prolegomena to library classification*. P. 68) and translate faithfully and faultlessly. To lay bare the specific subject of every book in this way would be a tortuous and wasteful task without the aid of the matrix supplied by the scheme of classification. All this preliminary analysis for the enunciation of the specific subject in the form demanded by the classificatory language, is 'Canalisation'. True translation depends almost entirely upon correct canalisation.

234 *Translation Proper*

Once canalisation is completed and the name of the specific subject settled by pouring (so to speak) the properly selected, prepared and amplified words of ordinary language into the mould made with the aid of Phase- and Facet-Analysis, the final step is a simple affair of substituting from dictionary (schedules) — occasionally with the aid of grammar (rules) — equivalent ordinal numbers for the selected words. This last step is translation proper. It is here that real metempsychosis takes place — the same soul appears in a new body, the old one having been made of words and the new one being made of ordinal numbers.

235 Advantages

Classificatory translation has some advantages over literary translation. It is, therefore, easier to become an adept in the former than in the latter, although a correct understanding of the substance and familiarity with the subject are equally essential in both.

2351 Apprehension Mechanised

While ordinary translation too involves a preliminary canalisation (transposition — or *anvaya* as it is called in Sanskrit), its matrix is not as rigid as that of the classificatory one. While its plasticity has a value of its own as indicated in section 231, it is less powerful in mechanising apprehension.

2352 Flaccidity Avoided

In ordinary translation great vigilance is required to avoid falling into allied processes of paraphrase, adaptation, imitation, even perhaps unconscious parody. The unwary translator may fall victim to them even in the stage of canalisation. But the austere precision of a classificatory language makes such vices of translation almost impossible. The translator will rather err on the side of too great terseness or meagreness then towards flaccidity or elaboration.

2353 Ambiguity Removed

A classificatory language, itself entirely without vagueness or ambiguity, removes them from the 'text' it translates. But this will work smoothly only if the Canons of Enumeration and Context (*Prolegomena to library classification*. Pp. 69-72) receive full attention in the work of translation. In the dictionary of a classificatory language, the arrangement of words is not alphabetical (which has no relation to sense) but filiatory or systematic as determined by sense. Thus the very position of every word enables the translator to keep clear of all ambiguity.

2354 Fixity Secured

Usage in ordinary language continually changes — sometimes suddenly (for example during wars or other great historical crisis) but for the most part imperceptibly, so that the translator can hardly take note of it. But a classificatory language is designed to stop such changes absolutely. This again greatly reduces the diffi culties of translation.

2355 Identical version Assured

There is a lengend that 70 Greek translation of the Hebrew Scriptures, each of them shut up in a separate cell without any sort of communication, produced verbally identical versions. Nothing short of the inspiration of the Holy Ghost indeed can explain this. But a classificatory language makes this miracle the norm: every translator (classifier) who uses the means provided will arrive at the same result (class number): translation has been made a science.

236 Imponderable Missed

The advantages of a classificatory language are in fact scientific advantages. Its matrix shapes the name of the specific subject as mechanically as the microtome cuts sections of protoplasm. It evidently fails where artistic (let alone inspired) translation succeeds in transmitting the imponderable: all that belongs to atmosphere and personality evades its formal net. Besides these general qualities there are also certain classes of books which classificatory language cannot define.

2361 Message Mocks

There are for example books with a message. They abound in Religion and Literature but may also occur (according to its own canons) in any subject that is treated from the centre with sufficient power and insight. They are seminal books. Here are some examples:

1 Newton (Isaac). *Principia.*

2 Darwin (Charles). *Origin of species.*

3 Steiner (Rudolf). *Problems of world economy.*

They are so fundamental and dynamic that they open new vistas of thought. It is beyond the power of classificatory language to bring out their seminal quality. It is no doubt a mockery when a classification scheme obliges the classifier to give them the same class number as for ephemeral text-books ostensibly covering the same main class, like

1 Bowley (Arthus). *A general course of pure mathematics from indices to solid geometry.*

2 Scott (George G.) *The science of biology.*

3 Thomas (S. Evelyn) *Elements of economics.*

The Colon Language has managed to separate the seminal books in a subject from the others by its Classic Device. (Chapter 7 of Part 1 of *Colon classification*).

2362 Flair Flouts

Then there are books written with flair — so alluring that it is we who are devoured by them: they so capture us that we turn their pages as if they were pages of time itself. Here are some examples:

1 Hogben (L). *Mathematics for the million.*

2 Wells (H.G), etc. *Science of life.*

3 Cole (G.D.H.). *The intelligent man's guide to the world chaos.*

It is such books written with extraordinary vigour that make reading popular. When classificatory translation stands flouted by their flair, there is no denying that it has failed miserably.

2363 Orientation Outwits

Then there are books more and more valuable nowadays, that orient the reader among specialised subjects whose inter-relations are dealt with nowhere else. Here are some examples:

1 National Council of Teachers of Mathematics. United States. *The place of mathematics in modern education.*

2 Thomson (J. A.) *Introduction to science.*

3 Kirckpatric (E.A.) *Sciences of man in the making.*

Quite apart from the needs of a man of general culture, such books may lead the specialist into wider horizons. It is no doubt sad that a classificatory language should be outwitted by the orienting quality.

2364 Standard Stupefies

There are of course dry-as-dust, merely mechanical, books of all sorts and standards. There is no means of fixing a standard for standards. They vary from time to time and place to place. We have only to compare the books prescribed for the same level of examination in the different universities at intervals of say a hundred years. To make confusion worse confounded the publisher takes law into his own hands and himself marks a standard. There is again the disturbance caused by the language of exposition apart from the difference in the level of ideas. One has finally to ask how many standards are to be recognised. Does standard grow by jerks so that we can count the number or does it grow continuously and present a spectrum which defies enumeration? In such bewildering circumstances how is one to judge standards absolutely? The question of standards appears to stupefy even the experts in the field of knowledge concerned. At a meeting of an august academic body, lists of text-books were once presented for examinations for the same year. A young, wary fellow pointed out that the same book found a place in the lists prescribed for examinations of totally different standards. The experts were apparently so stupefied that they voted down his proposal that the lists concerned may be rectified and brought up later. No. Classification should not get itself entangled with this will-o-the-wisp of standard. The Colon and the Decimal Languages dare not face them — not that the question of standards is immaterial — but because it is so elusive. In *Library administration* (1945) this question has been passed on to administration and the use of temporary extra-classificatory 'Sequence Symbols' to be added above class numbers and to be changed from time to time.

237 *Imponderables Evaded*

If a classificatory language cannot, it also need not distinguish books according to their more subtle qualities. That is the work of the reference staff. These have to be appraised differently for different readers according to the subtle traits of their own. It is a rule of the game of life that service to living man should at the ultimate stage be done only by living man. Mechanical aids stop short of that stage. It is like the rule of the game in hockey that the ball should be put into the goal only by one who is inside the ring. This does not mean that he should do all the running up and down the field passing the ball at all times from stage to stage. If the other players do all this efficiently, the one inside the ring will have the necessary freshness to do his job unerringly. The other players therefore fulfil themselves by making everything ready for the man inside the ring to attend to the ultimate act without any distraction or prior wearing out.

238 *Fulfilment*

So it is with classification. Classificatory translation has fulfilled itself as soon as books have been in every other way fully individualised and arranged in the most helpful filiatory order and made more usable by their mnemonics. This lays them ready to the hand of the reference staff whose business it is to match their untranslatable human qualities with their reader's needs. When the reference staff succeed in it, the library fulfils itself. This final fulfilment is best assured when the classificatory language attains its own fulfilment.

24 *Individualisation*

Viewing a system of class numbers as constituting a language with qualities mentioned in section 21 of this chapter involves a responsibility. And that is to find a unique, close-fitting, individualising class number for each specific subject. So long as the unit to be classified was a book, usually embodying knowledge of considerable extension, this responsibility was lightly borne and easily discharged. But if the unit to be classified turns out to be an article of tiny extension but great intension, *i.e.* if it is microscopic thought-units and not macroscopic thought-masses that are to be classified, the responsibility becomes severe and exacting. It becomes so difficult that one's mind develops all kinds of escapist or defence mechanisms. It prescribes "Be minute, be minute, but not too minute" as a guidance. It fixes *ex-cathedra* a ceiling for the number of digits in a class number as another mode of escape. Even those, who recognise the challenge which microscopic thought-units throw at exact documentation work, seek to pay homage to the escapist attitude by a mock concession to the resistance to individualisation induced by intellectual indolence in the majority in the profession.

241 A sop

For example, they feel obliged to offer a sop — or is it an apologia -- as the introduction to the fourth international English edition of *Universal decimal classification* (1943) does through the words:

"For administrative purposes, it is frequently advantageous to have specifications much more complete than those given, for example, in a catalogue to which the public have access. Over-elaboration of code numbers confuses an unskilled user of a public catalogue. For general library subject catalogue purposes, the class number selected should be as brief as will allow the book classified to be segregated within a reasonably small group, say not exceeding 20 to 30 references. For shelving purposes, an even broader classification can be employed without disadvantage, for the reason that intercalation of books is not so simple as intercalation of cards in a catalogue".

"Public", "Unskilled user", "Public catalogue" — all these imply a library of books embodying macroscopic thought-mass. Such books will admit only of "brief" class numbers. "Over-elaboration" will be denied by the books themselves. Class numbers needed to individualise them will generally constitute only "broader classification". It is all automatic. Why this grave and solemn warning?

242 A Trivial Reason

The next reason offered is trivial. It is argued, "If the classes used are too minute, spaces must be kept on the shelves at very frequent intervals to accommodate prospective accessions."

243 The Correct Note

The correct note is, however, struck in the next sentence asking of indolent colleagues for "hands off" from libraries where alone individualisation will need "over-elaboration of code numbers". It is asserted with firmness:

"Librarians of the specialist type, which are concerned mainly with articles in periodicals, or with similar documents relating to various specific subjects, need all the detail which is provided in the Universal Decimal Classification for the precise specification of these documents".

"Precise specification" is equivalent to "individualisation" of the embodied thought, which will be secured by the use of "brief" numbers in the case of books and "over-elaborate" numbers in the case of articles. Each will get what it deserves from a well-designed classificatory language. There is no need either to have different classificatory languages for the two purposes or to harp on the need for a wilful mutilation of the classificatory language if it has been so designed as to be capable of individualising microscopic thought-units.

244 Next Stage in Evolution

The next stage in the evolution of library classification is exploring the means for securing individualisation of thought-units in every conceivable region of the field of knowledge. Hitherto the classification of many of the arts and crafts had been left undeveloped as there was not much of published literature on them. But the situation is rapidly changing. They have all begun to attract considerable "articles in periodicals or similar documents". These subjects need to be fitted with appropriate Facet-Formulae to facilitate translation into classificatory language. Further, the older subjects — the academic subjects, the fundamental ones — are being burrowed deeper and deeper and extended in all directions. This calls for sharpening of old foci and formation of new foci. Classificatory thought must now be turned on these problems. More powerful notational devices and for this purpose far subtler principles must be discovered.

25 *Facetisation*

251 *Principle of Inversion*

In the construction of facet-formula, the Principle of Inversion must be borne in mind. This principle was discovered when Messrs. A. J. Wells, Bernard I. Palmer and myself spent a whole Sunday in July 1948 at Chaucer House, London, trying to come to terms with the problem of fitting some new subjects with facet-formulae.

2511 *Starting Point*

We started with the principles enunciated in the *Elements of library classification* (1946) as helpful in deciding Helpful Order of materials on library shelves and of entries in library catalogues. One of the principles has been named Principle of Increasing Concreteness. In Botany, for example, it is helpful to put the materials on relatively abstract specific subjects like Anatomy, Physiology and Pathology in general, before those on the relatively concrete specific subjects dealing with particular groups, families etc. of plants. In Education, it is more helpful to put relatively abstract subjects like Teaching Technique, Organisation and Measurement in general, before the relatively concrete subjects like Elementary Education or Education of Children, Secondary Education or Education of Adolescents, Adult Education and so on. Or again, in Law, it is more helpful to give priority to the general principles and treatment of different branches of law over the legal systems of particular communities which are of a more concrete nature.

2512 *Proof*

Assuming that this principle is to be followed in shelf-arrangement, what we observed was that the Facets in a Facet-Formula should be arranged in the inverse order i.e. according to the Principle of Decreasing Concreteness. To prove this we have to remember that the connecting symbol between two facets should have an ordinal value which is less than that of all the digits used to represent substantives. The proof will be facilitated if we work with a known system of notation which implements facet-analysis. Let us work with the notation of the Colon Classification. Here the connecting symbol is ":" and the digits which represent substantives are Arabic numerals other than "0" and Roman Capitals. Their ordinal scale is

: , 1 , 2 , ... 9 , A , B , ... Z

Take T Education. It admits of the two facets E or Educand and P or Problem. E is more concrete than P and, as it has been already stated, the books on pure problems must come earlier than the books on concrete classes of educands.

Consider the subjects

1 Secondary Education (= 2);

2 Educational Organisation (= 8);

The second of the above should come before the first.

Let us consider the facet-formula with P prior to E *viz.*,

T [P] : [E]

In the first subject, the Problem Facet is vacant, and so its class number is T:2

In the second subject, the Educand Facet is vacant and its class number is T8. Arranging the subjects l he ordinal values of their class numbers we get the order

T:2 Secondary Education

T8 Educational Organisation

which is not the order we wished to have.

If we reverse the order of the facets *i.e.* follow the inverse Principle of Decreasing Concreteness, we get

T [E] : [P]

By this formula, Secondary Education is T2 and Educational Organisation is T:8. Arranging the subjects by the ordinal values of the class numbers, we get the order

T:8 Educational Organisation

T2 Secondary Education

which is just the order which we wished to have.

It may be remarked that if we had decided that the materials should come on the shelves in the order of Decreasing Concreteness the Principle of Inversion would arrange the facets in the facet-formula in the order of Increasing Concreteness.

252 *Fundamental categories*

We come last to a fundamental point bearing on Facet-Analysis. An examination of the facets of different subjects shows that they can all be related to one or other of five fundamental categories: Time, Space, Energy, Matter and Personality. Any analysis ultimately strikes root in them. A student of advanced classification will, therefore, be helped if he becomes familiar with their existence in the background and gets his ideas clarified in regard to them.

2521 *Time*

Let us begin with time. It is perhaps the most abstract of all the five. The Chronological Facets in the main classes Geography, History, Economics and Sociology and the only Facet of Stratigraphy are instances in which the fundamental category Time figures directly and to represent itself.

We shall see later that it may also occur to represent the category Personality.

2522 *Space*

Space is perhaps more concrete than Time but not as much as the other categories. This fundamental category figures directly and to represent itself in the following Facets:

(1) The Space Facet in Geometry;
(2) The Geographical Facets in the main classes Geography, Economics and Sociology; and
(3) The differential Geographical Facets following the divisions 'Publications in a geographical area' of the Bibliographical Facet in Bibliography.

We shall see later (Section 25252) that it may also occur to represent the category Personality.

2523 *Energy*

The category Energy is much more ubiquitous than any other. There is hardly any class which does not have a Facet to correspond with it. The classes Engineering, Agriculture, Medicine, Animal Husbandary, and Sociology have even two Facets to correspond with it.

A Facet in which Energy figures directly and to represent itself is generally called Problem Facet. It is so in Library Science, the several canonical classes of Mathematics, Physics, Geology, Useful Arts and Philosophy, the main classes Chemistry, Technology, Biology, Botany, Zoology, Medicine, Mysticism, Linguistics, Religion, Psycology, Education, Geography, History, Political Science, Sociology and Law. In Sociology, the second Facet corresponding with energy is called Secondary Problem Facet.

In other classes the Facet corresponding with energy is called by other names: Bibliographical Facet in the class Bibliography.

Work and Secondary Work Facets in Engineering.

Farming, Operation, etc. Facets in Agriculture.

Handling etc. Facets in Medicine.

Veterinary and Handling Facets in Animal Husbandary.

Economic Facet in Economics.

2524 *Matter*

We meet with comparatively little of abstraction and a good deal of concreteness in the category Matter. We may recognise different grades of concreteness in describing matter by the terms Matter, Substance and Commodity. In the last mentioned, it is worth recognising two sub-grades: Intermediate Commodity and Ultimate Commodity.

All the visible things in our room belong to the category Matter. The 'Matterness' is common to all of them; it distinguishes them from Time, Space, and forms of Energy like Heat and Light. In regard to 'Matterness' all the visible things are alike and undifferentiable. In this undifferentiated, abstract form Matter figures only in the State of Matter Facet of Physics.

We can readily distinguish the different things in the room by the substance of which they are made — say Wood, Iron, the stuff of our own Body, and so on. These are matter differentiated into Substances. They are a more concrete form of matter. Substance Iron for example figures in the window gratings, the paper weight, the iron safe and so on. In regard to 'Ironness' these are alike and undifferentiable. In this undifferentiated form of substance, matter figures in most of the divisions of the Substance Facet of Chemistry.

The differentiated Commodity form — intermediate and some ultimate ones – figures in the Substance Facet of Technology. The rest of the Ultimate Commodity forms of matter figure in Useful Arts.

In the Ultimate Commodity which is the most concrete form of Matter, the 'individuating particularities' are so many that it is more appropriate to group it with the category 'Personality', if we can, for want of suitable terminology, force this word to represent not only Human Personality but everything — Human, Animal, Vegetable or Inorganic or other categories like Languages and Religion — which have an individuality and aroma of their own.

2525 Personality

The fifth fundamental category Personality, which has to be used in a very generalised sense as stated above, is unanalysable. We have to treat it gently and as a whole. It is the most concrete category.

25251 Figuring Directly

In the Educand Facet of Education and the Entity Facet of Psycology, the names of the facets use terms suggestive of human personality.

In the Group Facet of Sociology, the name of the facet uses a term suggestive of Social Personality.

In the Organ Facet of Medicine the name of the Facet uses a term suggestive of the physical aspect of human personality.

In the Natural Group Facets of Botany and Zoology and the Crop and Animal Facets of Agriculture and Animal Husbandry, the names of the facets use terms suggestive of the physical aspect of the personality of living organisms, other than man.

The Language Facet of Linguistics is concerned with the subtler personality of Language. So it is with the Religion Facet of the main class Religion.

In all the above cases, the foci in the facets are enumerated *ad hoc*. We shall now give examples of the foci of personality facets being the same as those enumerated in facets of other categories.

25252 Figuring Through Space

In History, the Personality of the national group studied is individualised, not by special or *ad hoc* numbers, but by Geographical Numbers, with the result that the Facet itself is called Geographical Facet. It must be remembered, however, that the category Space figures in this Facet not to represent itself but to represent one form of the category Personality. We may also say that Personality figures in this facet indirectly through the category Space. It figures in a similar indirect way in most of the divisions of the Community Facet of Law.

25253 Figuring Through Space and Time

The category Personality needs the joint services of Time and Space to get individualised in certain cases. When the Personality is that of an Institution, a Conference or a Commission, it figures indirectly through the combined categories of Space and Time in the Geographical and Chronological Facets of the common subdivisions *h*, *p*, and *t*.

The subtler form of Personality called style in Fine Arts similarly figures indirectly in the combination of the Geographical and the Chronological Facets of that subject.

25254 Furthest Reach of Concreteness

Lastly we come to the main class Literature. Here the highly evolved, fully differentiated, unique Personality of an author figures indirectly through the combined categories of Personality of another kind, Energy and Time represented in the Language, Form and Chronological Facets respectively. The even subtler Personality of a literary piece needs the services of all these three and to their combination, another Facet called Work Facet with *ad hoc* foci, has to be added to get it fully expressed. We get the furthest reach of concreteness here.

2526 Order of Arrangement of Categories

Several of these five fundamental categories may figure with Facets of their own in many classes. The question of the order in which the facets are best arranged is a delicate one. The Colon and the Decimal Classifications often arrange them in the same order. Occasionally, they differ as in regard to Style in Fine Arts and to Legislature, Executive, etc., of different countries. It would be a good exercise for the more ambitious students to list the cases in which they agree and those in which they differ and discover the fundamental principles, if any, which lie behind their respective practices. Such an exercise will give them practice in recognising different degrees of concreteness and abstraction. Though experience thus gained will not be quite necessary for elementary classification, it will be of help in advanced work both as classifier in dealing with multi-phased and many-faceted specific subjects and as classificationist in meeting fundamental difficulties that may be mobilised against him by the new subjects that get created from time to time.

253 Need for Research

A more objective and certain means of

(1) isolating the facets of a new specific subject;

(2) relating them to the five fundamental categories; and

(3) determining their relative order of concretness

may be found after enough experience is gained in fitting facet-formulae to several specific subjects by the method of trial and error. Considerable research and experiment is necessary to rescue this problem from dependence on flair and bring it to an objective scientific level.

254 Example of Facetisation

Here is an example of fitting a Useful Art with facet-formula. This is taken from a talk given by Mr. A. J. Wells under the auspices of the Aslib in London in November 1948. The Useful Art taken for illustration is

MX041 = Package manufacture

The facet formula suggested is

MX041 [P] : [M] : [F]

i.e. Package Manufacture [Part] : [Material] : [Fabrication]

Fabrication is a process and is therefore abstract. The Material used in the manufacture is certainly more concrete than fabrication. The Part of the package which is shaped out of the materials has attained a more concrete status than the material itself. It has indeed developed a personality of its own. If this is remembered and the Principle of Inversion is applied, we see the appropriateness of the above mentioned facet-formula. Let us reduce the facets to the fundamental categories. Fabrication is action; it is the manifestation of the fundamental category Energy in the context of this Useful Art. Material is of course the manifestation of Matter in the context of Package Industry and so it is more concrete. Part is the manifestation of the fundamental category Personality in the context of the industry in question. It is thus more concrete than Matter itself.

26 *Formation and Sharpening of Focus*

Whenever a facet-formula is constructed for a new subject, the foci in each of the facets must be formed. The first step within each facet is to fix a set of co-ordinate foci in the array of the first order; the next step is to fix co-ordinate foci in the arrays of the next order which can be formed from each of the foci of the first order. These will all be foci of the second order with reference to the point and so on.

Two processes are condensed so as to appear as one when we state: "foci must be formed" or "fix a set of co-ordinate foci in the array." In the latter for example, the first process is to enumerate the divisions of the first order — of course so as to be mutually exclusive and totally exhaustive — and arrange them in a helpful order. The second process is to assign ordinal numbers to them in keeping with that helpful order. If we can enumerate the divisions in a totally exhaustive way, the work of assigning digits may perhaps be simple. But what usually happens is that we can enumerate only a few divisions and in many cases only one, since the others are unknown for the moment. When new divisions come to light later, the new and the old divisions will together ask for a particular order among themselves as a helpful order. This will happen as and when new foci come to be written upon. If we give digits to each division arbitrarily so as to be according to the order asked for on each such occasion, the digits may have to be changed now and again in their denotation.

261 *A Fundamental Question*

Can we avoid this contingency — this difficulty? This question really amounts to this: When only a few or even only one division in the new array to be formed is known, can we so decide the digit by which it would be represented that it need not be changed when new divisions in the array come to be known? When only one division in the new array to be formed is known, we simply say that the focus has become sharper. The question is: When a focus becomes sharper, are we to sharpen its number by the addition of any digit arbitrarily, in which case it is liable to be contrary to helpful order when another division in its array appears and sharpens the original focus to the same degree? Or is there a particular digit by which its number can be sharpened without such a liability to change? The answer to the latter question is of grave import. If the answer is in the negative, there will be frequent changes in class numbers. If the answer is in the affirmative, two conclusions follow:

(1) there will be greatest permanence in class numbers and this is obvious; and

(2) all classifiers will grasp it *i.e.* fix the same digit, and this is welcome.

But it raises the fundamental question how is that particular digit to be known? This question can be answered and has been answered in certain cases. How the particular digit is to be known depends on the principle which will be most useful in choosing helpful order among the divisions likely to be formed in the array in question.

262 *Principles for Determining Helpful Order*

In this connection it will be of use to recall to mind the various principles by which helpful order may be determined among an array of co-ordinate classes. These principles may be taken from out of the six principles stated in the *Elements of library classifica-*

tion (1946). The first principle — the principle of decreasing extension — is concerned with a chain of progressively subordinated classes and not with an array of co-ordinate classes. The second principle — the principle of increasing concreteness — is concerned with the arrangement of facets and not with the classes in an array since abstract classes and concrete classes cannot go into the same array. The principle of canonical or traditional order does not arise, as by assumption we are dealing with a newly formed array. The principle of evolutionary order also is not of avail, since it does not carry with it definite stages applicable in all cases and cannot, therefore, suggest definite digits to represent definite stages. This principle can be of use only when all the foci in the array are known at once. But by assumption, they are not.

263 Chronological Device

Of the remaining two principles, the principle of chronological order is easy to apply and provides infinite hospitality in array, if it is relevant. The use of this principle to determine the number for a new focus of the first order or the additional digit to be added to sharpen an old focus has been called Chronological Device in the Colon Classification. The most happy use of it is in the individualisation of authors in the main class Literature. Here the number is uniquely determined for each and every author and everybody will arrive at the same number and the hospitality in array is literally infinite. Here are some examples:

Examples

In the *Colon classification,* we find the following rules: "O31 The number of the author of the literary piece or work which the book contains or about which the books treats or of the literary author about whom the book treats is to be placed immediately after the Form Number. This group of digits may be termed the Author Number.

"If the book is a biography or a criticism of, say, a poet, it is the poet who will determine the Author Number and not the author of the biography or criticism. For example, in the case of 'G. K. Chesterton's Innocence of Father Brown' Chesterton will determine the Author Number but in the case of the book 'G. K. Chesterton's Charles Dickens' it is Dickens and not Chesterton that will determine the Author Number. In order words, we must recognise what may be termed Author Inequality, *viz.*,

Author of Work (is not equal to)
$\neq$ Author of book

"O32 The Author Number is to be constructed by the Chronological Device, the Chronological Number being worked out to three digits and the year of birth of the author being used as the epoch."

According to these rules we can get class numbers for any of authors dead, living or yet to be born. The classifier can fix them by himself without waiting for any direction or decision by the classificationist. Here are some examples of living authors in English fiction (=O:3). The third column gives the Universal Decimal Number for later reference.

Colon Number	Author	Universal Decimal Number	
O:3M74	Maugham (Somerset)	82—3 (Maugham)	"1874—"
O:3M94	Huxley (Aldous)	82—3 (Huxley)	"1894—"
O:3N00	Hilton (James)	82—3 (Hilton)	"1900—"
O:3N04	Greene (Graham)	82—3 (Greene)	"1904—"
O:3N07	Du Maurier (Daphne)	82—3 (Du Maurier)	"1907—"

Moreover, an author who figures in many forms of literature will get the same notation in all the forms. For example

O:2M74	Maugham as a dramatist	82—2 (Maugham) "1874—"
O:3M74	Maugham as a novelist	82—3 (Maugham) "1874—"
O:6M74	Maugham as a prose writer	82—4 (Maugham) "1874—"
O:9xM74	Maugham as a literary critic	

Even in the latest edition of the *Decimal classification* we find only

823.91 Early twentieth century 1901 — [novelists]

It is not therefore possible for a classifier to assign individualising numbers to living authors. Even when the editors of the scheme work out such numbers, they can individualise only eight authors. The others that are already born and are yet to be born have to go unclassified i.e. unarranged in a helpful order. Moreover, an author who figures in many forms of literature does not get the same notation in all the forms; for example, we find

821.74 Scott (Walter) as a poet
823.72 Scott (Walter) as a novelist
824.79 Minor prose writers amidst whom Scott will have to be lost without individualisation.

It must be remembered that the distinctive digit which represents Scott is 4 in 821.74 and 2 in 823.72

In the Universal Decimal Classification, individualisation is got by using the surname of the author and his dates too if necessary as shown in the third column in the table of the five novelists given already. The Universal Decimal Numbers would throw the authors in an alphabetical order. For recreative reading this order may be helpful. But for critical and comparative study, the chronological order secured by the Colon Classification by the use of the Chronological Device will be more helpful.

264 *Geographical Device*

The principle of geographical contiguity is also easy to apply if it is relevant, though not as easy as the principle of chronological order. The use of this principle has been called Geographical Device in the Colon Classification.

Many of the languages not belonging to the three families — Indo-European, Semitic and Dravidian — are individualised by this device. As such languages are used in smaller areas and as they are not well-known and are only now beginning to attract books, it is only slowly that the need to individualise them arises. The Geographical Device enables everybody to arrive at the same number to represent them. This has been used also in determining the numbers of the less known religions which are prevalent in small areas and the literature on which is beginning to appear. Here are some examples:

Both the Colon and the Decimal Classifications prescribe the places where Geographical Device may be used. For example we find in the Group Facet of Y1 Sociology of *Colon classification:* —

7 Race as a social group

74 — 79 To be divided by the Geographical Device.

So also we find in the main class 57 Biology of the *Decimal classification:* —

572 Ethnology

572.9 Races divided by countries like 930—999

265 Subject Device

There is also another principle called Canon of Consistent Order and enunciated in the *Prolegomena to library classification* (1937): —

"Whenever the same set of divisions occur in different arrays, their orders should be the same in all such arrays, wherever insistence on such sameness does not violate other more important requirements."

Conformity to this canon will be conducive to economy of time and of attention or mental energy. It will minimise load on memory both for the classifier and the user.

It is the first aspect of this canon in the form "arrange the same group of classes in the same order, whatever be the array in which they occur" which is responsible for certain practices in some of the printed schemes of classification.

This use of this principle amounts to the use of the Subject Device. This is prescribed extensively in the Colon Classification and in the Decimal Classification. Here are some examples:

We find in the Business Facet of X Economics in the *Colon classification:* —

9 Other business (industries)

Divisions by the Subject Device *(Illustrative)*

9F182 Steel

9F551 Coal

9J Agriculture

9M13 Paper

9M7 Textiles

So also we find in the main class 33 Economics of the *Decimal-classification:* —

331.137 Unemployment
331.1378 By industry
82 — 899 may be divided like 620 — 699 with 81 divided like the whole classification for other industries e.g.
331.137822 Unemployment in mining
331.1378177 Unemployment in photography

266 *Unscheduled Mnemonics*

What about the cases where none of the above three devices is relevant or applicable? It is in meeting these remaining cases that the Colon Classification has something to show. What it has to show occurred involuntarily and unconsciously when the scheme was first designed. But an objective study of the scheme pursued in the *Prolegomena* disclosed that a subtle something had characterised the categories represented by the respective digits 1,2,3 . . . . . 8. For want of a better expression, that subtle something has been described as Unscheduled Mnemonics.

Following the usage brought into vogue by Berwick Sayers and others, representation of the same idea by the same number, wherever it may occur, is described as Mnemonic use of notation. The Geographical, Chronological and Subject Devices are obvious means of securing Mnemonics. As the digits representing Geographical, Chronological and Subject Divisions are already scheduled in a scheme, the Mnemonics secured by their use are called Scheduled Mnemonics.

In Unscheduled Mnemonics, there is no such recorded schedule to compel mnemonic use of digits, mechanically. On the other hand in order to be aware of it and to apply it, there is need to develop a subtle sensitiveness to recognise certain primordial patterns which inhere at great depths below the diversity of their manifestations in the phenomenal world and in arrays of co-ordinate divisions in facets of subjects. To illustrate one such pattern, we have

Structure, Function, Fault in structure or function and Correction of fault.

In the biological sciences, these manifest themselves and are denoted by the terms

Morphology, Physiology, Pathology and Remedy.

In sociology these manifest themselves as

Social structure, Social activities, Social pathology and Correctives.

By Unscheduled Mnemonics is meant the representation of these parallel ideas or analogues in the biological sciences and sociology by the same digits. In the Colon Classification, the digits used are

2 Structure and its analogues
3 Function and its analogues
4 Fault and its analogues
6 Correction and its analogues

2661 *Service of Gestalt Value*

In the natural language, there is no common term (word) by which all the analogues can be denoted. The classificatory language provides however a common term (digit) by which they can all be denoted. What exactly the digit means in natural language when it occurs in a particular subject, is determined by its Gestalt Value in its class number. When the number of the particular subject occurs in the Gestalt, it has merely to be read with the name of the subject so that the notation in question yields the meaning of the digit appropriate to the context. For example,

in I:3 Plant physiology, 3 is Physiology;
Y172:3 Primitive social activities, 3 is Social activities; and
P12:3 Latin syntax, 3 is syntax.

2662 *Reason for Failure to be Scheduled*

Mr. A. J. Wells has asked me more than once to clarify this Unscheduled Mnemonics and make it thoroughly objective. Some people impatiently and cynically brush aside the problem saying that it is all "too mystical". Some even make this an occasion to have a fling at the "Mystic East". The sincere asking by thinkers like Mr. Wells has been driving my thought deep down. While I am still unable to make it thoroughly objective, I have now found one reason for failure: it is due to an unequal fight between classificatory language and natural language. The latter does not have a term but the former has, to denote a certain idea. This reminds one of a statement of Goethe that a divine language alone can express the deeper experiences of a poet and that an expression in a natural language misses the depth, the aroma and the infinitude of experience. It is this incommensurability between idea and human expression which gives rise to the concept of mysticism. Ramkrishna Paramahamsa had said that he was eager to express to his friends that profound experience in his deep *Samadhi* state (usually translated as trance-state) which brought him supreme delight. But he remarked that, as he reached towards that state, the differentiated manifestations of the phenomenal world gradually shed their differences, and reduced themselves to fewer and fewer patterns, that when the number of patterns fell below a certain number they were so unfamiliar to the ordinary folk that the natural language, which alone was intelligible to them, had not thrown forth any term to denote them and that ultimately, when the pattern was about to be reduced to a single one, his own identity also was lost in the one; with the result, when he recovered from that depth, he could say nothing, in words intelligible to us, of experiences below a certain depth. The *Vedas* declare this in the well-known passage:

"Unable to reach which, the words return along with Manas".

Manas is that part of the mind which acts as a channel between *Chitta* (= memory) which is the store of impressions and experiences on the one side and *Buddhi* (= intellect) which develops the impressions and experiences by permutations and combinations and creates new impressions and experiences of its own. Production of articulate sounds, words and intelligible language, and other symbols, is one of them. As a transmission wire breaks down when the voltage increases beyond a certain measure, the *Manas,* which is like transmission wire between *Chitta* and *Buddhi,* is overpowered when the intensity of what is poured into *Chitta* increases beyond measure during deep experiences and *samadhi.*

2663 *Inference from Testimony*

What we gather, for our present purpose, from the testimony of poets like Goethe, realised souls like Ramakrishna, and the *Vedas*, is that an idea can and does exist without a word to denote it in its bareness and purity, though when viewed in the context of different particular subjects, its different contextual transforms do get expressed by different words. It is the translation of all such equivalent words into one and the same digit which is sought by Unscheduled Mnemonics.

2664 *More Patterns*

Here is another contextual interpretation of some of the digits already mentioned when used in some other subjects: —

In History and Political Science

(Structure) 2 Parts of the Government Constitution
(Function) 3 Functions of government
(Fault) 4 War and military activity

In Religion

2 The sacred books (which set the mould — distinctive form)
3 Theology (which represents its mode of correct functioning)
4 Religious practices, creeds etc. (which are the results of petrifaction, encrustation and other faults)

In Linguistics

2 Morphology
3 Syntax

As stated in section 214, the relation between the digits of a classificatory language and the words of a natural language is on the one-many kind. Here are some other patterns: —

The digit 3 may denote the following analogues: Analysis in Mathematics; Analysis in Chemistry; Metaphysics in Philosophy; Characters of Consciousness in Psychology; etc.

The digit 5 may denote the following analogues: Liquid state in Physics; Petroleum in Technology; Sap in Botany; Blood in Medicine and Zoology; Oceanography in Physical Geography; etc.

The digit 5 may also denote the following analogues: Flowers, Aesthetics, Women, Emotion, Glandular system, etc.

The digit 5 may also denote the following analogues: Ecology, Environment, Outside, Foreign Land, Alien, etc.

The digit 7 may denote the following analogues: Magnetism, Personality, Ontogeny, Composition, Literary sources in history, etc.

Examples

(1) Let us pursue the case of Package Manufacture given as an example of Facetisation in section 254. Mr. Wells has used the principle of Unscheduled Mnemonics in fixing the foci in the Fabrication Facet. Here are the illustrations: —

2 Making; with 21 Moulding; 22 Extending; etc.

Because these are deciding the structure, the digit 2 had been selected.

4 Faults

Here the mnemonics is obvious.

5 Decoration

This is in accordance with the second set of analogues given above for the digit 5.

7 Filling

This is the operation which leads to the fulfilment of the purpose of the package and it is at this stage that it attains to the fulness of its personality. The digit 7 had, therefore, been selected.

(2) The following passage, occurring in p. 32 of the booklet *Colon system and its working* (1944) by K. M. Sivaraman, is worth quoting:

"He (the classifier) can enjoy even a greater measure of autonomy if he has attuned himself to the unscheduled mnemonics implied in the Colon Schedules and illustrated in pages 129—133 of the *Prolegomena to library classification*. Then he can sharpen foci and even fit up new ones with appropriate numbers. To give but one example, 'Y 1 : 49 = Other Social ills' is not fully subdivided in the schedule. When a book on 'Refugee problem' was given to the class last week, all the students hit independently on Y 1 : 495 as its number as the digit 5 is the unscheduled mnemonic for "Water, Liquid, Ocean, Foreign Lands, Aliens and External environment".

"Classifiers endowed with greater power and fired with more ambition can even venture to determine the facets and the foci appropriate to them in the endless cannonical classes of Useful Arts as they attract more and more of literature. It would be wise however that the result at this level is not finally fixed without collaboration by the classificationist."

(3) In the Organ-Facet of the main class Botany, we find the focus 16 Flower among the sharper foci of 1 Regional organs. The next recorded focus is 17 Fruit, which is co-ordinate with 16 Flower. Recently a book dealing exclusively with Pollen arrived in the Delhi University Library. It was R. P. Wodehouse's *Pollen grains etc.* Since Pollen is a part of flower, the focus 16 needed sharpening. Since the function of pollen is to help phylogeny forward and since phylogeny is one of the analogues represented by 6, the number for Pollen was fixed as 166. In fact, the 6 in 16 Flower had itself been fixed on the same basis.

2665 *Cognate Foci*

When the same digit is invoked for sharpening a focus more than once *i.e.* when more than one focus in its first-order-array has claim for one and the same digit, these foci are assigned to different octaves in that array. These may be called Cognate Foci. Generally speaking, the focus assigned to the first octave is believed to attract more literature to itself than the one assigned to the second octave. Similarly the latter is expected to attract more literature than the focus assigned to the third octave and so on. There may thus be a parallelism of unscheduled mnemonics in the different octaves even as there is a parallelism in the quality of the notes in successive octaves of the musical scale. And the Octaves are generally speaking in decreasing order of Bibliographical Richness even as there is a decreasing order of intensity in the secondary, tertiary etc. spectral lines in Raman Spectra. In general, this order will be the same as the order in which the Cognate Foci come to be written upon.

Example

The book *Earth, radio and the stars* by Halen True Stetson described its scope as "the directed study of the relation of the earth to the cosmic schemes" which is bidding fair "to introduce us to a new science '*Cosmecology*' ".

This being a book on Astronomy (=B9), the prescribed facet-formula is

B9 [B] : [P]

i.e. Astronomy [Body] : [Problem]

The focus in the Body Facet is Earth and it is already scheduled. We are to consider the focus in the Problem Facet.

The term 'Ecology' is not merely rhetorical. It is significant. The book deals with the use of the radar in obtaining information about the heavenly bodies which constitute the cosmic environment of the earth. In the Problem Schedule under B9 Astronomy in chapter B Mathematics, the focus Ecology does not occur. The third set of analogues given for the digit 5 in section 2665 suggests its representation by the digit 5. But the printed schedule has used 5 to represent Spherical Astronomy. This is no doubt in keeping with the same third set of analogues. Because, spherical astronomy is concerned with the positional study of the heavenly bodies in the cosmic environment of the earth. Spherical astronomy had come to be written upon from very early days and is already bibliographically quite rich. Its place in the first octave can not be grudged. It would therefore be graceful for the new arrival — Cosmic Ecology — to accept the analogous seat in the second row, as it were, *i.e.* it is fitting that this new analogue of 5 should be translated into 95. Thus, the class number of the book is decided to be B91:95.

2666 *Need for Research*

As I have already stated, it is not yet possible to put these across to others objectively in cold print bereft of the advantages of personal communication. By experience and personal transmission and above all by concentration and contemplation on the published schedules, the unscheduled mnemonics can be imbibed.

Surely if some research can be made into the subject and some kind of schedule can be constructed reducing analogues of different species to their respective fundamental patterns and the numbers representing them, a scheme of classification will give greater autonomy to individual classifiers and will therefore reduce the time-lag involved in *ad hoc* numbers having to be arbitrarily fixed by the headquarters of the scheme for every new formation in the field of knowledge; and this will bring reading materials on many such new formations instantaneously into the same kind of orderly organisation in all libraries and bibliographies.

We said in section 252 that the construction of facet-formulae can be objectivised by relating the facets and the characteristics of classification corresponding to them to the five fundamental categories: time, space, matter, energy and personality and by developing sensitiveness to recognise minute differences in the degree of concreteness or abstraction involved in two or more of a series of concepts.

So also, the formation of foci in new facets or of new foci in old facets and the sharpening of foci in any facet can be objectivised quite easily in certain cases by the use of Chronological, Geographical and Subject Devices. More can be achieved in this matter by a systematic reduction — of as many categories as possible of these as are likely to occur as foci in the different facets of the various subjects — to layer after layer of a smaller number of categories at successive depths until we reach a convenient number of fundamental patterns at a suitable depth — very much like what is done in Basic English. We should then denote them by appropriate digits and construct illustrative schedules of analogues. This will have to be done both by intellectual methods of tabulation and induction, and by intuitive methods. I have a feeling that help can be derived in this matter from some of the ancient lore like that of Chaldeans. In India, a good deal of symbolism had been developed in the past to express what is not easily expressed, if not inexpressible, in words. The *Bijaksharas* (= a system of alphabetical symbolism recorded in the medieval age) may give help. But they should be de-coded into modern language. By ignoring or suppressing such packets of intuitive knowledge, humanity has been, for a few centuries, giving intellect full opportunity to build everything in its own way. There is no doubt that we have gained a good deal from this. The Western countries have played a glorious part in this. We have reached a stage of atomisation of knowledge and thought that it is beginning to be a burden even for the ablest intellectuals. Can we say that the time has come to revive the intuitive, synthetic organisation of knowledge? Can the two modes of organisation be made to supplement each other without suppressing each other? Will this be one of the outcomes of the recovery of India, Asia and the East in general from centuries of exhaustion, inaction and stagnation? Will the world of learning be benefited in this way by the apparent preparedness of the West to co-operate with the East as equals and bring about mutual respect, understanding, co-operation, sympathy, and synthesis at all levels — material, mental and spiritual?

27 *Future of Evolution*

To summarise, facetisation and the scheduling of the deeper mnemonics which are now left unscheduled need to be made objective. This objectivisation is likely to happen in the near future as the next stage in the evolution of the fundamental or abstract aspects of library classification. The more this work evolves, the more effectively will classification begin to function as an international language for the exact and expeditious service of even minute units of thought and the greater will be the autonomy of individual classifiers. As and when a subject attracts books or articles to itself for the first time, it may be possible for a classifier to fit it with the correct facet-formula without waiting for instruction from the classificationist. As and when work in a subject is carried into divisions of greater intension, it may be possible for a classifier to sharpen the foci concerned without waiting for instruction from the classificationist. Moreover, there will be greater stability in the facet-formulae and the schedules of foci. The expectation of their life will be greater. The existing facet-formulae and schedules of foci for the fundamental and traditional subjects can be brought to a more rational basis. A definite procedure will evolve for the way in which the library profession and the other professions can co-operate and compare notes from time to time, and make classification keep step with work in every subject.

Chapter 3

LIBRARY CLASSIFICATION AND SOCIAL FORCES

31 Social Purpose of Library

Apart from the aesthetic joy which individuals may derive from its pursuit, library classification is essentially a product of social forces. That is because the library itself is a social institution charged with a set of social duties. These duties centre on one social purpose. That purpose is the activation of the human mind by the transmission of thought-energy across both time and space. Thought-energy gets created in the human mind and it is best transmitted through the whole personality of the one in whose mind it gets created. The immediate presence — the physical, visual, audible presence — of the creating personality is necessary for this. The ideal transmission can therefore reach only a limited few — the contemporaries who are near enough and can hear, see and feel. But society is spread out far wider in time and space, than can be reached in this ideal and most effective way. Alternative ways have therefore to be used, though they are less effective, even as we are obliged to use preserved, powdered milk when fresh milk is not available. One of the alternative ways is to transform thought-energy into a material, portable form which can be preserved for any length of time and transported across any distance. By preservation of the material, it can be made to reach posterity and posterity can re-transform it into thought-energy and get its own mind activated by it. By transporting the material, it can be made to reach anybody anywhere in the world and he can re-transform it into thought-energy and get his own mind activated by it. This preservable, transportable state of thought-energy is, of course, the reading and kindred materials.

The duties of a library include the collection, organisation and administration of such materials so as to make them reach posterity as well as the contemporaries.

311 *Conflict of Duties*

As materials are perishable and perishability increases with frequency of use, there is an inherent conflict between these two duties. To reach posterity is to restrict use among contemporaries and to reach contemporaries is to restrict use among posterity. This conflict between two duties had led to emphasis being laid more on the one than on the other. The emphasis has also shifted from the one to the other as changes have occurred in the factors which determine the emphasis. One of these factors is the availability of reading materials — the ease and the cost of their production and reproduction to restore what perishes by use. Before the invention of printing, books were neither cheap nor easily produced. There was therefore an involuntary preference to preserve them rather than to shorten their life by an aggressive campaign for their use. Preservation was therefore practised as paramount ever since writing was invented. It had been well ingrained in human nature — it had almost become a race-inheritance during the thousands of years before printing was invented. It is now five centuries since the invention of printing from movable metallic types made the multiplication of copies of a book so easy, quick and cheap that they can be discarded and replaced by fresh ones without heaviness of heart or undue cost as and when they get worn out by use. And yet it is only now after five centuries that the emphasis is evenly distributed in just a few countries between preservation for posterity and an unrestricted campaign for the widest possible use among contemporaries. In other countries there is still a blind resistance to this shift of emphasis.

312 *Resolution of the Conflict*

The concept of one dormitory library in each nation for preservation for posterity and a net-work of a work-shop type of libraries for ensuring use by one and all of the contemporaries has resolved the conflict. As the work-shop type of libraries are more numerous and make themselves more felt, it even appears as if the emphasis is now on service to contemporaries rather than preservation for posterity. But that is not true.

313 *Effect of Democracy*

This shift in the emphasis favoured by changes in the method of book-production has been intensified during the last century by the development of another factor. That is a social factor. It relates to the concept of aristocracy *versus* democracy. Democracy as equal opportunity to all to grow mentally, each in his way, at his own rate and to his own fulness, came to be increasingly recognised since the turn of the nineteenth century. The policy of throwing open libraries as much to the last man as to the first has come in the wake of democracy. Democracy appeared first in some of the Western countries and it was their libraries that were first thrown open. It is these countries which now abound in the work-shop type of libraries which seek to serve one and all with materials with which they can resonate most. Democracy is only now spreading in the other countries, whether of the West or of the East and their libraries too will soon be multiplied in number so that every person can have easy access to them.

32 *Effect on Classification*

These two mutually reinforcing factors — printing and democracy — which are transforming the outlook of libraries, are affecting library classification in a profound way. There is every evidence that this discipline is on the eve of entering its heyday as a result of the reinforcement of these two factors. It looks as if the new capacity which library classification will develop will profoundly affect even the way in which books and particularly articles now appearing in periodicals will hereafter be issued. Indeed the conference convened by the Royal Society of London in June last to consider the work of documentation, which turns essentially on library classification, and the mode of publication of articles which men like Dr. Burnell for example are comtemplating upon and advocating are not isolated phenomena or freaks. It is a symptom of the social forces that are lifting library classification to a higher stage of evolution somewhat like the one outlined in the second chapter. The resolutions passed at the conference are a harbinger of the tremendous revolution which is about to take place in library classification as a natural and inevitable consequence of the social forces in question.

321 Days of Broad Classification

In the earlier years, there were only a few books. Each book covered a large area of the field of knowledge. There was, therefore, need only for a broad classification. Those who used these books were mental giants. They formed the uppermost centiles of the community as arranged in the measure of their mental capacity. They were men of highly integrated personality, with acute intellect and capacious memory. There was therefore no need to mechanise the arrangement either of the broad classes of knowledge written upon or of the books in a class. There was thefore no social necessity to take classification to the second stage of evolution *viz.* development of an organic, expressive notation of ordinal numbers to represent the classes of knowledge or the books.

322 Beginnings of Notation

As printing advanced, an intensive cultivation of the field of knowledge was promoted by books and the division of knowledge covered by a book gradually began to shrink in extension and gain in intension. This meant that arrangement by a broad classification was no longer adequate. The number of classes had to be increased. The number of books also increased. The size of libraries too increased. The onslaught of democracy led to the admission of the masses into the library. Their intellectual acumen and capacity of memory were so diverse in character that it was no longer possible to find one's way with comfort or certainty amidst numerous books arranged alphabetically by author within a broad class, in order to find out just the books which had a bearing on the specific subject of one's interest. Democracy demanded that books should be arranged and displayed on the shelves as well as in the catologue according to the modulation of. their varying thought-contents. This compelled the number of classes to be increased to the extent demanded by the book-world. These were too many, for their order to be remembered verbally by the library staff. This made the denoting of the classes by a system of ordinal numbers a convenience if not a necessity. The initiation of the practice of attaching an elaborate and consistent notation to classification, during the seventeenth century and that too in France, was not a fortuitous occurrence. The intellectual ferment which led to the beginning of specialisation and the spread of printed books over diverse regions and depths of the field of knowledge in the seventeenth century, and the leading position which the French people were occupying in the promotion, absorption and spread of that ferment and of the wave of democracy, explain the emergence of library classification in that place and at that time.

323 Emergence of Dynamic Notation

By the time we reach the middle of the nineteenth century, old France had been exhausted and young America was bursting into activity. The Americans were not bound down by the chains of high-brow tradition like the older countries. Books came to be published on quite a variety of specific subjects. There was no privileged class to resist the spread of democracy and the equal-opportunity idea. Books had to be put across to the last man in as great a plenty and with as much expedition as to the first man. No subject was too low to be represented on the shelves of the library and no person was too low to be served by the library. "Ask Library Anything", said Melvil Dewey, "and that is American Library Association". It was therefore no accident that the first system of library classification with a dynamic, expressive, expansive notation, capable of receiving, digesting and featuring future knowledge, should have been invented in America in 1873 and should have spread to Great Britian and to the other older countries of the West. 1850 is an epoch in library history. That was the year in which public libraries began to figure widely in the legal system of humanity. 1870 is an epoch in educational history. This was the year in which compulsory, universal education began to figure widely in the legal system of humanity. At the crest of these times was thrown forth Dewey to carry library classification forward in response to the social pressure that was developing on libraries. Dull lethargic librarians resisted and ridiculed. Sensitive, sprightly Dewey marched forward and triumphed. The number of the classes needed went on increasing from 1,000 to 10,000, then to 100,000 and then beyond measure. The Decimal Classification expanded in equal measure upto a point. That point was reached in about 30 years.

33 Need for Nimbler Notation

That point was the one where a change took place in the world of readers and of reading materials. It is continuing now. Specialist readers have increased. They appear in the fundamental sciences, the applied sciences, the industries, the arts and crafts of all sorts and the newer social sciences. Specialisation has become so intensive that a specialist in one land can not find his peer or superior for exchange of thought and communion in an adequate number unless he swept the whole world. To provide for exchange of nascent thought among them, the periodicals being published in the world have increased a hundredfold in number. The thought-units embodied in the tiny articles scattered over them have become the staple food of a large number of specialists. World-economy demands that these articles should be organised and featured in a most helpful way so that to the eyes of every specialist, whatever be his focus of interest, the arrangement should appear as if it radiated from and irradiated his own focus. To effect this kind of arrangement, in spite of the surprise eruptions, mutations and hybridisations in the field of knowledge, it is no longer possible to use a notation which was forged against a background of macroscopic masses of knowledge embodied in books. A notation nimble and subtle enough to seize, isolate and display any microscopic unit of knowledge embodied in tiny articles, is needed. These elude the Decimal Classification. For this purpose, the Universal Decimal Classification has armed the Decimal Classification with some new notational devices and propped it up. It has been doing this work for about 30 years.

34 The Joint Drag of Democracy and Aristocracy

The triumph of Decimal Classification amidst the books in public libraries — libraries meant for the masses and used by them largely for recreation or general information — and the conceit and conservatism of the learned classes which created and acted on the slogan "classification is a logical absurdity", led to an untoward result. The powerful and highly organised personalities of the nineteenth century forming the university dons and members of learned societies could still manage to "know their materials" without notational help. They had temperamentally no resonance with those who were less gifted. Librarians of these bodies were usually drawn from that very superior class. They were not capable of so bending their aristocratic attitude as to worry themselves about the difficulties of the ordinary man in finding his way through a mass of published literature to pick out his materials. They never devoted much thought to library classification. Library classification had therefore to grow in the hands of librarians working in public libraries. These had three handicaps. In the first place, the Decimal Classification was so good that it anticipated most of the needs of a public library and inhibited further thought on classification. Secondly public libraries did not generally attract enough of men who had had the intellectual discipline and awareness that university life provides; and the sheer intellectual delight of pursuing a pure and fundamental technique for its own sake did not emerge in a sufficient number of them. Thirdly, the democracy which used the library did not, for long, go in for specialised study and the social pressure forcing the sharpening of classificatory technique in the right way was not incident on public librarians to an adequate degree. Thus the technique of library classification could not grow — due to neglect by librarians of learned libraries and lack of incentive and initiative among librarians of the libraries for democracy. The public librarians, who alone were numerous and well organised, were slow to perceive the change gradually taking place in the unit of classification from macroscopic masses of thought embodied in books to microscopic units of thought embodied in articles. With all the weight of the mass which organisation in a democracy gives, they persisted in their own ways of stereotyped courses of studies, examinations and routine in book arrangement and resisted a slowly emerging sensitive class of librarians whose very function was to organise microscopic units of thought embodied in articles. Such was the joint drag of intellectual democracy and aristocracy on the evolution of library classification.

35 *Emergence of Documentation*

The newly emerging sensitive class of libraries are those being established by wealthy industries. Although their number is small, they are able to command more money. The tension between the many and the few with money is becoming intense. The heat at the Lamington Conference of the Aslib in September, 1948, and the voting on the issue whether business librarians should be placed among librarians or scientists and technical workers, are a measure of this unfortunate tension based on passion which has nothing intrinsically to do with documentation and bibliography or classification and cataloguing or service to scientists and non-scientists; these are the same in all libraries, public, academic or business. The public librarians appear to underestimate the power of money and every attempt to pit their larger number of votes against the few who are working in business libraries stiffens the latter. Abusive sentiments develop in each group in the usual way. The latter think of the former as the vulgar mass; the former reciprocate by thinking of the latter as imperialistic dictators. They would not touch each other's terminology even. The public librarians have been using the term "Bibliography" to denote a list of writings on a specific subject and the art of making it. The business librarians would call it only by another name "Documentation". No doubt the bibliographies of the former were often made up of the titles of books with only a dash of articles. But still the technique of building it, arranging it and serving it is the same as for "Documentation".

351 *Pressure of Industries*

Bibliographical work began to make considerable progress under the label of documentation. There seems to be something in the name. A long-used name appears to wear out and lose the power to stimulate and attract. The industries are becoming sensitive to the usefulness of a good library and of documentation service. Tiny processes, details of commercial information, patents, minutest variations in processes, market conditions and designs and the latest developments in the fundamental sciences and the related or auxiliary fields, are coming to be valued. The industries insist that these are of the very essence of the service they expect of their library. This means that the classification and cataloguing used in documentation should be capable of isolating, individualising and throwing into helpful order microscopic units of thought.

352 *Pressure of Tradition*

The fact that a scheme good for the materials that had to be handled in the earlier epoch had established itself in many libraries and that an impressive notational prop of a more recent origin had prolonged its life, amounted to a tradition. As all other traditions, even this tradition began to exert its pressure, though it was only about half a century old. This pressure was reinforced by a drag created by the tradition of "Subject headings" which had to originate independently as soon as the classification scheme in wide use was overpowered by new subjects which it could not individualise. Above all the pressure of the industries had not become high enough to break these lingering traditions, to force a re-examination of the very foundation of classification to find out if it could stand the pressure caused by the change-over from macroscopic masses of thought embodied in books to microscopic units of thought embodied in articles, and to force an appraisal of the national and international waste involved in the ascertaining of the thought-unit of a material in quick succession by two different technicians — the classifier and the cataloguer — with two different probes and techniques and therefore often arriving at different modes of expressing it. During the last twenty years when the business libraries had been organising themselves independently, and the industries were unable to exert the pressure needed to think of a new foundation, many documentations had been built by the Universal Decimal Classification whose new attachments were so attractively elastic as to hide the rigidity of the Decimal Classification which it had indolently adopted as a readily available core. These very documents are now cited as an obstacle to admit the case for re-examining the foundations of classification or the wastage continuously involved in using independent techniques for classification and the determination of subject headings. A little reflection will show how irrational it is to argue that because we had been doing something in a particular way in the past and any change-over means trouble, cost etc., we should rule out all attempts to change. This argument will tie all future to a year of the past. That is not the way in which the world grows. The industries themselves do not grow that way. A costly machinery of 1949 is scrapped in 1950 to give place to a totally new design because it is more efficient. The industries do not hesitate to finance such a change-over. On the other hand they know that they will suffer if they do not change-over. The industries should take a similar view of the machinery of library classification also and provide the finance necessary to rebuild it. The library profession too should become more aware of the crumbling of the present foundations of classification, which still rest on arbitrary numbering at bottom, and put up a case for a re-design of the foundations in the light of the factors which led to its break-down and the methods of research and growth which prevail now and are likely to prevail in the future as far as they can be foreseen leading to new formations in the field of knowledge. The present foundation was the first which had ever been designed for library classification. It could not have been the best or the most enduring one. Considerable experience has been gained in observing its behaviour. There is every chance that one designed in the light of this experience will have a longer life and stand a higher pressure from the field of knowledge.

36 *Approach to New Foundation*

One possible approach to a new foundation has been indicated in chapter 2. It had been suggested by a critical and comparative study of the Colon, Decimal and other classifications in the set of the three books already referred to. It is based on a discussion of the problem in the class-room and in group conferences. The very genesis of the Colon Classification was due to a realisation that library classification was in need of being based on a foundation which reached down to a greater depth than the enumerative schemes known till then. This realisation was based on what was observed in British libraries about twenty-five years ago. A scheme which enumerated actual specific subjects was seen to develop cracks and get out-moded day by day. An enumerative scheme with a superficial foundation can be suitable and even economical for a closed system of knowledge. For example, such a scheme will work well for Ancient Greek or Indian Philosophy both of which had become crystallised and fixed in far-off days. They may even present a continuous spectrum of specific subjects. Even then they can be tied by an enumerative system as with a thong. It is not the mere infinite nature of the universe of knowledge which baffles an enumerative system so long as it is only a statical continuum. What distinguishes the universe of current knowledge is that it is a dynamical continuum. It is ever-growing; new branches may stem from any of its infinity of points at any time; they are unknowable at present. They can not therefore be enumerated here and now; they can not be anticipated; their filiation can be determined only after they appear.

The only course open is to find and enumerate the fundamental categories and the possible fundamental types of relation which can develop between them. By permutating the categories and the relations taken any number at a time, we can get a representation of the formations in the field of knowledge. The assumption is that suitable simple ordinal numbers can be so chosen to represent the categories and relations that a parallel permutation of all the parallel combinations of them will yield composite ordinal numbers whose order will correspond with a helpful order of the formations in the field of knowledge. If this assumption is correct, the foundation of a library classification can be safely laid by conceiving it as a language. In other words, a linguistic foundation is likely to be as stable as can be conceived for a library classification. The pressure of social development on library service has now reached a stage where the fundamental issue of examining the foundations of library classification on objective lines herein suggested or similar to these can no longer be evaded.

Chapter 4

LIBRARY CLASSIFICATION AS A TRANSFORMATION AND ITS LIMITATIONS

Let us assume that a linguistic foundation is laid for library classification, that the fundamental categories and types of relations have been isolated to the necessary and sufficient extent and enumerated and arranged in a helpful order, and that suitable ordinal numbers have been found to represent them. Then any specific subject will first be analysed into the fundamental categories which go to form them; then the types of relations involved will be determined; all these will be translated into their respective ordinal numbers and will then be finally assembled according to prescribed rules. This will be the class number of the specific subject. The presumption is that the class numbers which can be composed in this manner will all fall in a helpful order if they are arranged according to their ordinal values and that every possible specific subject of the past, present and future will be individualised by them. The question arises whether this order will be found to be helpful by every user. It will be if and only if there is one and only one order which is helpful to all users, and all other orders are totally unhelpful to every user *i.e.* if there is a sharp line of demarkation between helpful and unhelpful orders irrespective of the kind of user and only one order will lie on the right side of this line and all the others will lie on its wrong side.

41 An Example

Let us first examine some simple particular cases. Let us take the main class Psychology. For definiteness let us take that two facets occur in its facet-formula *viz.*

Psychology [Entity] : [Problem].

The resulting class numbers will first group the reading materials in psychology by the Entity studied. Let us for simplicity consider two entities only:

Genius and Idiot.

Let us assume that these are to be taken in the order given above. Then as a person approaches the psychology room in a library, the first gangway will have all the materials on Genius and the second, all the materials on Idiot. Of course, the materials in each gangway will follow the order of problems. Here again for simplicity let us consider two problems only,

Emotion and Conation.

This arrangement will be helpful to a person who specialises in a particular psychological type. But a person who specialises in a particular psychological problem will find that his reading materials are not found together. If he specialises on Emotions, he will have to pick up his materials from two gangways. So also if he specialises on Conation; if there are a hundred foci in the Entity Facet, he will have to pick them from a hundred different places. This will be unhelpful to him. The helpful order he will demand is that the materials must first be grouped by Problems — all materials on Emotion together in one gangway, all on Conation in another and so on. But if they are so arranged the specialist of the first kind will find the arrangement unhelpful.

Let us imagine a well-guided stock-room. When the first kind of specialist enters, he wants the gangway guides to show the names of entities like Children, Adolescents, Women, Genius, Idiot etc., so that he can walk into the gangway in which he is interested, say Genius. When he enters into it, he wants the bay-guides to show the names of several problems like Sensation, Character of Consciousness, Cognition, Emotion, Conation etc. following in helpful succession. When the second kind of specialist enters, he should be able to press a button; and the gangway-guides, bay-guides and the materials themselves should be thrown into a different pattern. The gangway-guides should now show the names of the Problems. If he enters the gangway of his choice, the bay-guides in it should show the names of Entities.

Unless there is provision for such an instantaneous change in the arrangement of the materials and the guides as in a kaleidoscope, both kinds of readers cannot be given an arrangement which is helpful to them.

42 *Multiplicity of Helpful Order*

In other words, the facet-structure of specific subjects makes more than one order among them equally helpful if we take the totality of the kinds of readers into consideration, though for each kind of reader there is one and only one order which is helpful and every other order is unhelpful. It may also happen that a reader does not always belong to one kind. His interest at one moment may be as for the first kind of reader and at another moment as for the second kind. Thus, even from the point of view of a single reader, the facet-structure makes more than one order among specific subjects equally helpful. The multiplicity of helpful orders is not the creation of library classification or of its notation. It is inherent in the relation of the field of knowledge and the world of readers. For the facet-structure is inherent in specific subjects whether a scheme of classification explicitly recognises them as the Colon Classification and the Universal Decimal Classification do or implicitly takes them into consideration in arrangement as the Congress Classification does generally or the Decimal Classification does in Subjects like Medicine and Literature but fails to do in subjects like Education. Interest in different orders of facets is also inherent in readers. Multiplicity of helpful orders is inherent also similarly in the phase-structure of specific subjects, the interest of readers in different orders of phases and therefore in the relation between the field of knowledge and the world of readers.

43 *Methods of Solution*

Since multiplicity of helpful order among specific subjects is a fact independent of library classification — a fact to be reckoned with in arrangement — how are we to provide for it? It is a case of arranging concrete materials — books and other kindred materials — in such a way that one kind of arrangement presents itself to one person and another kind to another person. To secure this by pressing a button is obviously possible only in the world of fancy; it is not possible in the world of reality. Real solutions to the problem were explored in 1942 when this was discussed closely in the class-room at the instance of Das Gupta who was then a member of the class. One mode of solution is to design the stack-room in a lattice-pattern. At each of the lattice-points, books on one and only one specific subject will be shelved. The very pattern allows gangways running on all the four sides of a lattice point. Let us, for definiteness, assume that one set of gangways run from east to west and another set from south to north. The guides of the east-west gangways show, let us say, the names of Entities and the guides of the north-south gangways show names of Problems. Readers will walk down the appropriate gangways according to their interest. Calculation shows that a stack-room of such a lattice-pattern will require floor-space many times larger than the stack-room of the lanepattern. This may be anything between 100 times to 1000 times or even more per volume according to the number of books which collect on each specific subject. This is obviously impracticable.

When the number of facets in a subject is three the number of helpful orders will be six. To provide for all the six helpful orders with equal efficiency, a much more complicated lattice-system in more than two dimensions will be required. The complication will increase tremendously with subjects which have four or more facets.

44 Solution by Multiplication of Copies

The first method of resolving the conflict, due to multiplicity of helpful order, being fanciful, the second being unrealisable on account of spatial extravagance and dimensional complication, we can think, as a third solution, of the purchase of as many copies as the number of helpful orders and make different libraries of them for the different helpful orders. In this case, library classification cannot be based on a linguistic foundation such as the one postulated, not allowing more than one class number to a book. If however purchase of the necessary number of copies is feasible, it may be possible to design a classification without such a restriction. Perhaps we may use a multiplicity of classificatory languages — or dialects of one and the same language — one for each of the parallel libraries to be formed. We must be prepared to face whatever new difficulties it may lead to. However finance will certainly rule out this solution.

45 *Knowledge is Multi-dimensional*

The problem appears to be insoluble for all practical purposes. That it is so can be shown by an analogy drawn from mathematics. Every facet and every phase in a subject corresponds to a dimension of it in a mathematical sense. For its extension, freedom and behaviour, one facet or phase is independent of what happens in any other facet or phase. Each specific subject may therefore be taken to be multi-dimensional. The ensemble of specific subjects, that is the field of knowledge itself, is therefore multi-dimensional. The field of knowledge covers the phenomenal world. The phenomenal world — in fact each phenomenon — is multi-dimensional. To comprehend it ideally, the mind must be capable of taking in many dimensions simultaneously. Most of our primary senses have evolved to the stage of taking in only three dimensions. The intellect however is able to comprehend many dimensions. Of late, mathematical discipline has so sharpened intellect that it has just become able to reach up to the concept of infinite dimensions as a limit of finite ones. Humanity has at intervals thrown forth supermen — Indian tradition call them *Rishis;* Frank Townshend uses the word *Urthmen* to denote a transitory type between solely intellectual men and the *Rishis* — with a mental feature — or is it supramental? — different from the primary senses and the intellect and capable of taking in infinite dimensions directly and unmediated by the limiting concepts developed by the intellect. Modern language has not yet finalised the term by which this factor can be denoted. Indian tradition uses the epithet *Ārsha* or *Divya* or *Tāpasa* to denote it. The term 'mystic experience', which unfortunately induces a sceptic attitude in many, appears to be the only English one which is gaining currency in describing that factor. First-rate poets like Valmiki, Shakespeare and Goethe are able to communicate to intellectuals some of their trans-intellectual experiences. Fully integrated persons like Jesus, Muhammad and Ramakrishna Paramahamsa are also able to do so.

46 *Library Classification as a Transformation*

But as classifiers our job is not to communicate multi-dimensional experience as a whole in its nascent form of thought-energy. Our work is to arrange the materialised forms of multi-dimensional thought, the embodiments of thought in books and kindred materials. The materialised forms of thought are to be arranged so as to be cognisable by the primary sense of sight, which cannot comprehend more than three dimensions even in the most favourable circumstances. There is indeed a further restriction imposed. For the arrangement of books has to proceed along a line only and even there in one direction only. A set of arranged books form a unidirectional one-dimensional set capable of being followed up by the eyes and handled by the hands in a sequential manner. At the same time they represent the multi-dimensional continuum of thought. Thus library classification is equivalent to a representation of a multi-dimensional continuum in a single dimension.

47 *Limitations of the Transformation*

Such a representation can not be unique. It will admit of several alternatives. The representation of any continuum on a continuum of a smaller number of dimensions will admit of alternatives. Take for example the simple case of representing three dimensional space on two dimensional space — the representation of the globe as a plane map. We know the difficulties of map-projection, and the alternatives we have to reckon with. If we choose a projection which keeps the proportion of areas invariant, the angles go wrong. If we choose a projection which keeps the angles invariant, the proportion of areas goes wrong. Between these two extremes there are many other alternatives. Users of maps know what a bewilderment this leads to. In the same way if we want the books in one facet or phase to cohere, those in another facet or phase are denied coherence. If an arrangement is made in accordance with what one interest deems helpful, the other interests find it unhelpful.

48 Need for Help from Catalogue

Library classification, which is subject to the mechanical, dimensional and financial restrictions such as we have, has irremovable limitations imposed on it by multiplicity of helpful orders among specific subjects. It is, as it were, a knowledge of this irremovable limitation inherent in itself which makes library classification look for help from outside. Some help is possible from another tool common among librarians, the library catalogue.

Chapter 5

LIBRARY CLASSIFICATION AND ITS SYMBIOSIS WITH LIBRARY CATALOGUE

The library catalogue offers in two different ways the help needed by library classification in the distress caused to it by multiplicity of helpful order.

51 Punched Cards

One is the mechanical way of punched card system which, as the name implies, is available only if the catalogue is kept in cards on the basis of "one book — one card". In this, the catalogue card of each reading unit, whether it is a book or an article, is punched all along its edges. The punched holes fall into groups corresponding to the facets of phases and each punched hole in a group corresponds to a focus in the corresponding facet or phase. The punched holes form in fact a code language like the raised points in a braille-book or the punched holes in a monotype-spool or in an automatic telegraph spool. The punch hole in each facet-group corresponding to the focus of the book in the facet in question is cut into a slit.

511 Example of Psychology

Let us take the case of books in psychology referred to in section 41 of chapter 4. Let us, for example, assume that the upper edge corresponds to the Entity facet. Each punch hole in it corresponds to a focus in the Entity facet. If a book is on Genius, all the other punch holes — say for Child, Adolescents, Women and Idiots — are left alone and the hole representing genius is cut into a slit. Let us further suppose that a side edge corresponds to the Problem Facet. If the book is on Emotion, all the other punch holes — say for Sensation, Cognition and Conation — are left alone and the hole representing Emotion is cut in a slit. A similar thing is done in the cards of all the books in psychology according to their respective foci in the two facets. The cards may be kept in any random order. If a reader wants the entries on Genius, a rod is first inserted through the punch-holes representing Genius in the upper edge of a pack of cards. These are by design in corresponding positions in all the cards. The rod is then raised. As it is raised, none of the cards which had its punch hole slitted will be lifted by it. These will be the cards on Genius and will be left behind while all the other cards will be lifted up since their punch holes are unslit. This is done for all the cards on Psychology, taking them out in convenient packs. The cards on Genius are thus mechanically separated and kept aside. In this way, for the first kind of reader who specialises on Genius, all the materials on his subject are brought together and to his notice. If he now wants these cards arranged by the problem, they are further sorted. For this purpose, the rod is pushed through the hole for Emotion in the side edge which represents the Problem Facet. Of course, the cards should be so turned that the side edge in question go up. As the rod is lifted, it lifts up only those cards which are not on emotion. Those on Emotion alone will be left behind. After making use of them, the cards can be put back into the cabinet without any attention to their order.

For the second kind of reader who specialises in Emotions, sorting is first done with the punch holes in the side edge and he will be helped with all the entries on Emotions. If he wants them sorted out by Entity and wants those on Emotion of Genius, another lifting through the hole for genius is made.

A symbiosis can thus be stablished between library classification and library catalogue by the method of Punched Cards.

52 *Chain Procedure*

In the second way, each book or article is given additional cards called Class Index Cards. The main cards are arranged by the class numbers. Their class numbers will throw them in one of the helpful orders. And so the kind of reader, who is in need of it, is straightaway put in possession of what he needs. The books and cuttings too are arranged in that order, so that he need not use the cards at all, if he is using books or cuttings. Of course, he must use the cards if they simply show location of articles in periodicals. This is however a trivial detail. Let us illustrate the help given to the other kinds of readers by the library catalogue through its class index cards.

521 Example of Psychology

Let us use the same particular case as before — the case of psychology. A book on "Emotion in Genius" has the two-faceted class number S61:5. This class number is thrown in the form of the following chain: —

S	= ↓	Psychology
S6	= ↓	Abnormals
S61	= ↓	Genius
S61:5	=	Emotion

By the chain procedure explained in the *Theory of library catalogue* (1938) and the *Classified catalogue code* (1945) and simplified in the *Library catalogue: Fundamentals and procedure* (1950), the book will get the following added entries known as class index entries: —

1 EMOTION. *GENIUS.*
See classified part of the catalogue behind the class number S61:5

2 GENIUS. *PSYCHOLOGY.*
See classified part of the catalogue behind the class number S61

3 ABNORMALS. *PSYCHOLOGY.*
See classified part of the catalogue behind the class number S6

4 PSYCHOLOGY.
See classified part of the catalogue behind the class number . . . . S

Similarly a book on the Emotion of Idiot will get the class index entries

1 EMOTION. *IDIOT*.
See classified part of the catalogue behind the class number S62:5

2 IDIOT. *PSYCHOLOGY*.
See classified part of the catalogue behind the class number S62

The third and the fourth entries for Genius will serve the case of Idiot also. Thus the reader of the second kind will look for his material under the heading Emotion. There will be many entries which give him the numbers giving the location in the classified part of the catalogue for the entries of all the books falling within his field. There will be as many locations as there are Entries beginning with Emotion and having for Secondary Headings the names of Entities.

A symbiosis can thus be established between library classification and library catalogue by the method of chain procedure. Symbiosis is reciprocal dependence. We call this relation between classification and catalogue a symbiosis, because not only the catalogue gives a helping hand to classification in matters where it is more competent but also classification gives a helping hand to the catalogue in the determination of the phases, facets and foci where it itself is more competent.

Thus the library catalogue can help library classification where it comes to a dead-end and feels overpowered by the occurrence of multiplicity of helpful orders. In either way of help, the facets and the foci are put to use by the library catalogue.

53 Comparison of the Two Ways of Help

It is not necessary for the Philosophy of Library Classification to go into the relative merits of these two ways in which library catalogue can give help. However, it is difficult to resist the temptation to examine this problem. A few remarks will, therefore, be made before leaving this chapter.

(1) In the chain procedure there is no limit either to the number of facets which it can handle or to the number of foci in each of the facets.

But there is a physical limit in regard to these, set by the size of the catalogue card in the punched card system.

(2) In the chain procedure, the time-lag between demand and supply is only the time taken by the reader to look up his heading in the alphabetical part of the catalogue, to note down all the class numbers to which he is referred, and look up each of them in the classified part.

In the punched card system, the time-lag is the time taken for the mechanical handling (by the staff it may be) which will be greater if the catalogue is beyond a certain size.

(3) In the chain procedure, the time taken for the writing of the added class index entries will be greater than the time taken to slit the punches in the punched card system.

Between the greater loss of time at a time when the staff works behind the screen in the chain procedure and that once for all for each book when it is admitted into the library and not after the reader has appeared on the scene, and the greater loss of time at a time when the staff works in the presence of the reader *i.e.* after the reader has put in his demand — and this will recur with each reader —, the Fourth Law of Library Science will prefer the former.

(4) In the chain procedure, more cards will be required and more cabinet space too than in the punched card system.

The Fifth Law of Library Science will egg on the Law of Parsimony to prefer the latter way.

(5) In the chain procedure, the catalogue cards will always be orderly and usable for administrative and other purposes, whereas they will be always disorderly in the punched card system.

It appears that the Second Law "Every reader his reading material" will be equally satisfied with either of the ways in which the library catalogue can pull library classification through its difficulty. But it has to be carefully examined if the Fourth Law "Save the (subjective as well as objective) time of the reader" will not prefer the chain procedure to the punched card system. Again what is the verdict of the Fifth Law "A library is a growing organism" which implies also growth in the number of facets which subjects can have and the number of foci which can occur in each facet? This is what the first of the five statements of comparison given above is concerned with. The implications of this statement should be carefully examined.

Chapter 6

THE CAPACITY OF A LIBRARY CLASSIFICATION EMANCIPATION OF ORDINAL NUMBERS

Brevity is one of the qualities prescribed for classificatory language in category 53 of section 215 of chapter 2. The briefer the class numbers, the greater the convenience. The length of a class number is equivalent to the number of the digits making it up. If we remember that the numbers are all decimal fractions the number of digits needed to construct a number of given ordinal value will depend on the stock of digits we have at our disposal, that is on the number of digits which form the basis of the number-system — in other words, on the base of the notation. The longer the base of the notation, the briefer will be the numbers. This phenomenon is well known in Arithmetic.

61 Capacity for Class Numbers of Specified Length

The following table gives the number of specific subjects which can be given class numbers whose length is specified for different lengths of the base of notation:

Number of digits in Class Number	No. of digits in the Base of notation: 1	2	3	10	D
1	1	2	3	10	D
2	1	4	9	100	D^2
3	1	8	27	1,000	D^3
4	1	16	81	10,000	D^4
5	1	32	243	100,000	D^5
.	.	.	.	.	.
10	10	1,024	59,049	10,000,000,000	D^{10}
.	.	.	.	.	.
n	1	2^n	3^n	10^n	D^n

The number in each cell gives the number of specific subjects whose call numbers have the number of digits shown at the beginning of its row, when the number of digits in the base of notation is the number shown at the top of its column. If we denote the number of digits in the class number by *n*, the number of digits in the base of notation by D and the number of specific subjects in question *i.e.* the number of possible class numbers by $s\ (n, D)$, we have

$$s\ (n, D) = D^n$$

D^n is the measure of the capacity of class numbers with *n* digits, when the base of notation has D digits.

62 *Capacity for Class Numbers not Exceeding Specified Length*

The following table gives the number of specific subjects which can be represented by class numbers which do not contain more than a specified number of digits for different lengths of the base of notation.

No. of digits in the Base of notation

Upper limit for the Number of digits in Class Number	1	2	3	.	10	.	D
1	1	2	3	.	10	.	D
2	2	6	12	.	110	.	D^2+D
3	3	14	39	.	1,110	.	D^3+D^2+D
4	4	30	120	.	11,110	.	$D^4+D^3+D^2+D$
5	5	62	363	.	111,110	.	$\frac{D^6-D}{D-1}$
.	.	.	.		.	.	
10	10	2,046	88,572	.	11,111,111,110		$\frac{D^{11}-D}{D-1}$
.	.	.	.		.	.	
n	n	$2^{n+1}-2$	$\frac{3^{n+1}-3}{2}$	.	$\frac{10^{n+1}-10}{9}$		$\frac{D^{n+1}-D}{D-1}$

The number in each cell gives the number of specific subjects, the number of digits in whose class numbers does not exceed the number shown at the beginning of its row when the number of digits in the base of notation is the number shown at the top of its column. If we denote the maximum permissible number of digits in a class number by n, the number of digits in the base of notation by D, the number of specific subjects in question by C (n, D), we have

$$C(n, D) = \frac{D^{n+1} - D}{D - 1}$$

C may be called the capacity for the specified length of the base of notation and the specified upper limit to the length of class number.

The capacity of a library classification is thus a function of the number of basic digits it uses and the upper limit which it imposes on itself regarding the number of digits in its class numbers. From the point of view of capacity, a library classification is determined by these two numbers: D and n. This shows that there are two ways in which the capacity of a library classification can be increased *viz.* by increasing D or n. The table in 62 shows that increasing D by 1 increases the capacity more than increasing n by 1. Using the notation of Finite Differences

$$\frac{\Delta C}{\Delta D} > \frac{\Delta C}{\Delta n}$$

It can be conjectured from this that it will be an advantage to make D larger than n.

621 *Principle of Increasing Return*

The form of the function for the capacity of a library classification shows that the rate of its growth increases with D as well as n. Indeed it gallops with a tremendous acceleration. It is the Principle of Increasing Return that we meet with. This means that the addition of one extra digit to the base of notation increases the capacity tremendously if the base is already fairly long. The acceleration itself increases as D increases. Therefore the need or the desire to lengthen the base will be very meagre after the base has reached a certain length. The longer the base, the more meagre will be the need and the tendency to add even one extra digit to it. This will have a wholesome effect on classificationists.

63 *Upper Limit to* n

Various considerations suggest an upper limit to *n*, the number of digits in a class number.

631 *Books*

In the case of books, the class number has to be tooled on its spine or written on a tag affixed to it. The normal width of the spine of a book is about an inch. This suggests 10 or 12 as the upper limit for *n* and 5 or 6 would be convenient. There is an irony here. Compendious books which cover a large range of knowledge usually have a broader spine but call only for short numbers. It is the thinner books of the monograph type which deal intensively with a narrow range of knowledge that need long numbers. When Decimal Classification was designed, it was compendious books which were dominant and even with a small base of notation, it was possible to individualise most of the subjects embodied in books with class numbers of less than ten digits. But, of late there is a contraction in the range of knowledge embodied in books. Specialised books are increasing in number. This calls for the use of a longer base of notation in order to keep the number of digits in class numbers within bounds. It has been said that the joy brought to a grammarian by the saving of a fraction of a phoneme is as much as the birth of a son would bring. So it is with those engaged in designing schemes of classification. It is this urge which accounts for a long enough base of notation.

631 *A Warning*

There is another way in which some classificationists seek to satisfy this urge. That is to sacrifice the obligation to individualise a specific subject, in order to keep the length of class number within bounds. This results in assigning one and the same class number to a whole chain of distinct but subordinate classes — to give the same number to all of them as for their immediate universe *i.e.* the major class of which they are all subclasses. Of the two evils — the one of sacrificing individualisation and the other of admitting irritatingly long class numbers staring us in our face — it is desireable to tolerate the latter. In that case, the long class numbers will always be reminding us of their existence and we will be made to invent some more powerful notational devices to shorten the numbers. If we tolerate the former evil, there will be nothing visible to show that we had succumbed to an evil and to make us improve the capacity of the library classification. When one of two alternative evils must necesserily be accepted, we must use discretion in the choice. The epic *Ramayana* has a delightful episode to emphasise that wisdom lies in putting aside prestige and choosing that form of evil which shows explicitly and permanently the measure of our failure. In the war between the hero Rama and the anti-hero Ravana, Ravana who was prestige-ridden threw away all the dead bodies of his force into the sea. Rama did not do so. At the end of the war, a herb was brought into the battlefield by a medicine-man, the perfume of which revived all the fallen. Rama's men got up as from sleep; but, alas, the bodies of Ravana's men were not there to get the benefit. And so let us make the results of our short-comings stare us in our face and stimulate us to further effort.

632 *A Higher Limit for Documentation*

Apart from this warning that individualisation is paramount in classification and that it should not be sacrificed to shortness of notation, there is the fact that the length of class number crosses the comfortable limit more often in documentation than in book-arrangement. In documentation, the restriction imposed by the spinewidth of the book does not arise. Apart from the absence of this physical restriction, the mental resistance to long numbers is likely to be less in those who habitually seek and use documentation service. They will be men of higher calibre. They may tolerate longer numbers. A higher upper limit may, therefore, be allowed in documentation work for the number of digits in class numbers. In other words, the capacity of the library classification may be increased by increasing n rather than D in order to meet the demand of documentation.

64 *Emancipation of Ordinal Numbers*

The search for longer base of notation usually lands one on an alphabetical base. The change-over to such a base implies the unconscious acceptance of the letters of the alphabet as ordinal numbers. It implies also an unconscious acceptance that an ordinal number need not have a cardinal analogue. Unfortunately the traditional use of the same digits and words to denote cardinal and ordinal numbers had curtailed the freedom of the latter. The mathematician's pre-occupation with cardinal numbers had led to his neglect of ordinal numbers. One of the bye-products of the emergence of library classification as a discipline resulting in an artificial language of ordinal numbers is leading to a conscious emancipation of ordinal numbers. The base provided by the letters of the Roman alphabet has been used by the Colon Classification to lengthen the base provided by the Arabic numerals. In fact, the base of lower case letters is taken to be smaller in ordinal value and the base of capital letters to be greater than the base of the numerals. Making allowance for the omission of *i* and *o* which are inconvenient to use, the base of notation has thus been extended from 10 to 50. A statistical study of the length of class numbers recorded in section 5129 and its subdivisions of the *Library classification: Fundamentals and procedure* shows that this expansion of the base of notation has resulted in making the capacity of the Colon Classification reach with 5.3 only as the average number of digits in class numbers, the capacity which the Decimal Classification attains with 7.4 as the average number of digits in class numbers. It is able to individualise many more subjects by adding two more to the average number of digits and bringing it to 7.2 which is still less than that of the non-individualising Decimal Numbers.

641 *Connecting Symbols*

The emancipation of ordinal numbers from the thraldom of cardinal numbers leads to the emancipation of the base of notation from the thraldom of the traditional symbol groups. It provides freedom to take, wherever necessary, symbols from outside traditional groups and interpolate them in the base at the places where they are needed. We have already seen in chapter 2 that apart from substantives, conjunctions are needed to represent different kinds of relations. The Universal Decimal Classification has utilised, for this purpose, the result of the emancipation of ordinal numbers and introduced relation-signs like :, / . (.) " " and so on. It is true that it has not explicitly either called them ordinal numbers or defined their ordinal values. None the less, these are all implied in the notation of that classification. In the Colon Classification, the connective symbols are all deliberately conceived as ordinal numbers and their ordinally values are defined in exact terms.

642 Peculiarity of Conjunctions

It happens that all the ordinal numbers devised for connective purposes lie between 0 and 1. In the second edition, : and — were devised. In the forthcoming fourth edition, which is working out the details necessary to meet the requirements of documentation work, additional conjunctions are being introduced. They too lie between 0 and 1. Zero itself is only a conjunction in the Colon Language. From this it has to be conjectured that a digit which is a conjunction by itself or is the first digit of a conjunction is to have an ordinal value which is less than that of any digit which is a substantive.

Chapter 7

INCREASING OF DIMENSIONS AND OPTIONAL FACETS

Documentation work calls for close classification, even according to those who do not speak of individualisation or have not realised the importance of avoiding homonyms in classificatory language. Moreover, many specific classes of great intension which figured only in documentation work yesterday get embodied today in independent pamphlets, monographs and books. This phenomenon in the world of reading materials suggests that the same library classification should be used both for books and documentation work.

71 *Increase of Dimensions*

Documentation work has to individualise articles of deep intension. Their specific subjects have many more dimensions than those of books. A dimension really means a facet or a phase, so that the above statement means that more facets and phases are called for in documentation work. Let us take as a concrete example some specific subjects of great intension belonging to Library Science. To make the argument itself concrete let us try to translate them into Colon Language introducing provisionally various facets and foci, and changing the existing facet-formula from 2 [P] : [L] to 2 [L] : [P] in anticipation of what is being contemplated to be done in the forthcoming fourth edition. That is, we shall take the facet-formula as

Library Science [Type of library] : [Problem] instead of
Library Science [Problem] : [Type of library]

Here are 27 specific subjects some of which show additional facets separated by a dot instead of by a colon: —

1. 2	Library science
2. 2:75	Documentation service in libraries
3. 24	Business libraries
4. 24:75	Documentation service in business libraries
5. 248	Library of Government departments
6. 248:75	Documentation service in Government departmental library
7. 248:75.*m*2	Documentation service of pamphlets in Government departmental library
8. 248:75.X9F183	Documentation service on steel industry, in Government departmental library
9. 248:75.X9F183.*m*2	Documentation service of pamphlets in steel industry in government departmental library
10. 248.*a*M3	Government departmental library in 1830's
11. 248.*d*3	Government departmental library of Great Britain
12. 248.*d*3:75	Documentation service in government departmental library of Great Britain
13. 248.*d*3:75.*m*2	Documentation service of the pamphlets in government departmental library of Great Britain
14. 248.*d*3:75.X9F183	Documentation service on steel industries in government departmental library of Great Britain
15. 248.*d*3:75.X9F183.*m*2	Documentation service of pamphlets on steel industries in government departmental library of Great Britain
16. 248.*d*3.*a*M3	Government departmental library in Great Britain in 1830's
17. 248.W023	Parliamentary library
18. 248.W023:75	Documentation service in parliamentary library
19. 248.W023:75.*m*2	Documentation service of pamphlets in parliamentary library
20. 248.W023:75.X9F183	Documentation service on steel industries in parliamentary library

21. 248.W023:75.X9F183*m*2	Documentation service of pamphlets on steel industries in parliamentary library
22. 248.W023.*d*3	Library of the British Parliament
23. 248.W023.*d*3:75	Documentation service in the library of the British Parliament
24. 248.W023.*d*3:75.*m*2	Documentation service of pamphlets in the library of the British Parliament
25. 248.W023.*d*3:75.X9F183	Documentation service on steel industries in the library of the British Parliament
26. 248.W023.*d*3:75.X9F183.*m*2	Documentation service of pamphlets on steel industries in the library of the British Parliament
27. 248.W023.*d*3.*a*M3:75.X9F183.*m*2	Documentation service of pamphlets in steel industries in the British Parliament in 1830's

The above class numbers are using some of the devices which are being experimented upon to reconcile deep-level classification with autonomy for classifiers. The chief features of the experiment will become clear as we proceed with the notes on the above numbers. The first six class numbers are normal. They are just like what we come across in the book-world. They have one or two facets. They can grow in one or two dimensions independently of each other. The rest have more facets. Let us take the twenty-seventh example which has the greatest number of facets. It has freedom to grow in seven dimensions. It seems that when the focus in the Library Facet is 'Government Departmental Library' and that in the Problem Facet 'Document Service' the facet formula may be written as

2 [L] . [D] . [G] . [C] : [P] . [S] . [M]

i.e. Library Science [Type of Library] . [Department] . [Geographical Area] . [Chronological Period] : [Problem] . [Subject] . [Material]

72 *Optional Facets*

Here, the first three and the last two connecting symbols between facets are dots instead of colons. We may first explain why this change is made. Suppose all the connecting symbols are colons. Then by rule a colon must be retained even though the facet that it introduces is vacant. The result will be that a number of consecutive colons will appear if some of the facets happen to be vacant. For example,

The number in the second example would have been 2:::75

The number in the fouth example would have been 24:::75

The number in the sixth example would have been 248:::75

The number in the seventh example would have been 248:::75::*m*2

This accumulation of colons will be very inconvenient. The class numbers to be put on ordinary books used by ordinary readers will have to carry the load of so many colons because the class numbers of the specialised pamphlets and articles, of interest only to a handful of specialists, need them for the proper individualisation and organisation of the materials concerned. Hitherto classification schemes did not seek to individualise specific subjects like those given as the twenty-seventh example, which have definite foci in all the seven facets. We have now to individualise them for documentation service. The ordinary way of individualising them would subject the class numbers of ordinary non-specialised books being covered with a heavy debris of colons. We were eager to satisfy the specialist as well as the ordinary reader. We examined if we could not add extra temporary dimensions in between or after the dimensions prescribed in the normal facet-formula. In other words, we desired to provide for Optional Facets. We called them optional in the sense that if any of them were absent, we need not indicate its absence by retaining its connecting symbol. We have postulated the possibility of this and designed a dot as the connecting symbol for an Optional Facet. We have found that its ordinal value should be so fixed as to lie between ":" and "—".

This device enables us to spread out the class number into more dimensions than those prescribed by the facet-formula (= formula for compulsory facets) whenever a specific subject demands it, without humiliating those that do not demand them by a remainder that they are lacking in dimensions, by the accumulation of connecting symbols. A facet-formula with optional facets inserted may be called an Amplified Facet Formula.

73 *Autonomy for Classifiers*

This device no doubt gives freedom for class numbers to grow at several additional points. But, if nothing more is done, the schedule of classification will have to swell to enumerate every possible optional facet for every specific subject and to enumerate the foci in every such optional facet. This would take away one of the merits of the Colon Classification *viz.* slimness of schedule. What we are now investigating is whether we can not give greater autonomy to classifiers and also preserve the slimness of the schedule — in other words, whether we cannot leave the determination of the optional facet and the foci in them to the discretion of the classifier and yet be sure that all classifiers will arrive at the same facets and arrange them in the same order.

Here is found one helpful feature. To use the terminology of chapter 25 of *Library classification: Fundamental and procedure,* it turns out that all the compulsory facets are differentiating facets and all the optional facets are differentiated ones.

This means that each focus in a compulsory facet will call for its own distinctive optional facets to follow it. What these are will be made clear by the specific subject which has them and we are concerned in knowing them only if they have them actually.

At this stage, we have to consider two distinct problems which will be caused by the multiplicity of optional facets available to be attached to a focus in a compulsory facet. These problems must be solved by some suitable prescription if the autonomy of classifiers is not to lead to synonyms and destroy one of the essential qualities of a classificatory language.

74 *Order of Facets*

The facet-formula given towards the end of section 71 shows that the focus "government departmental library" in the Library Facet can have three Optional Facets attached to it *viz.* Department, Geographical Area and Chronological Period. The class number of the twentyseventh example has all the three. The first problem to be considered is whether all classifiers can be led by rules to arrive at one and the same order of these optional facets. Our conjecture is that they can be. Every classifier will arrive at the same formula if he observes the Principle of Inverse Order *i.e.* the Principle of Decreasing Concretness in arranging the facets in the facet-formula. To do this, he must develop, by practice, sufficient sensitiveness to varying degrees of concreteness. A general guidance will be to find their analogues among the fundamental categories — Personality, Matter, Energy, Space and Time — and be guided by the assumption that these fundamental categories have been mentioned above in decreasing order of concreteness.

Let us illustrate. Let us assume that X61 = Currency and that the facet-formula for it is

X61: [P] : [G] : [C]

X61: [Problem] : [Geographical Area] : [Chronological Period]

For example, "Demonetisation of currency in India in the 1940's" will be translated into X61:791:2:N5

Now consider "Demonetisation of thousand rupees notes in India in 1940's"

Here two new ideas have come in: —

(1) Denomination of the currency, (2) Material of the currency, which we may denote by D and M respectively.

These should be interpolated as optional facets after X61. The question is in what order we should take them. "In the order of decreasing concreteness", is the guiding principle. To decide the relative concreteness of D and M, we must find their analogues among the fundamental categories — Personality, Material, Energy, Space and Time. It is denomination of a currency that fixes its individuality and hence its analogue is Personality. The material of which it is made is the analogue of Matter. Thus, the two optional facets should be taken in the order D and M. Thus the Amplified Facet Formula becomes in this case.

X61. [D] . [M] : [P] : [G] : [C]

We must observe whether there are cases of extremely subtle difference in the dregree of concreteness and provide some guiding rules to make the correct decision in such cases. This is a piece of work that awaits to be done to avoid exhaustive enumeration of optional facets and the vesting of greater autonomy in classifiers.

75 Class Numbers with Only One of the Optional Facets

Consider the class numbers of the tenth, eleventh and seventeenth examples, with two more similar ones added: —

They are respectively

248.*a*M3	Government departmental libraries in 1830's
248.*d*3	Government departmental library in Great Britain
248.5	Library of publicity department of Government
248.W023	Parliamentary library
248.X09	Library of Ministry of Labour

These have ony one optional facet. But they are all different ones They are in fact Chronological, Geographical and Departmental Facets respectively. The notation has been so designed that they fall in the above order. We must investigate what would be the most helpful order and design the notation accordingly. The order is conditioned by the digit which immediately follows the dot. The digits 1. . . 9 A. . . . . Z have already the subject values assigned in the schedule of main classes. Canon of Consistent Order requires that we must preserve their order and it also means that the numbers of an optional facet which begin with digits should be deemed to have been constructed by the Subject Device. The only other digits which can come immediately after a dot are the 24 lower case letters. It is contemplated that these 24 letters may be divided suitably among the five fundamental categories: Personality, Matter, Energy, Space and Time. Experiments are to be made to decide the most helpful allocation of the letters among them. In the provisional examples given above *d* is assigned to space, *a* is assigned to time.

751 Distribution of lower case letters

Let us examine why they are so assigned and in general how the lower case letters should be distributed among the five fundamental categories. For this [illegible] with the usual assumption that on the shelf we prefer increasing order of concreteness. We shall then consider the five cases like those given in section 75 where only one optional facet occurs and choose the five cases in such a way that the optional facets in them have as their analogues a different one of the five fundamental categories. Then it follows that the one with the optional facet having time-analogue must come first, the one have space-analogue must come second and so on until the one having personality-analogue comes last. This shows that the earliest group of the lower case letters should be assigned to Time, the second group to Space, the third to Energy, the fourth group to Matter and the last group to Personality. It is on this principle that *a* has been assigned to Time and *d* to Geographical Area in the examples of section 71. How many distinctive analogues will arise for each of the five fundamental categories, how many of the lower case letters should be assigned to each category and if they prove insufficient to represent all the analogues, what other symbols can be added to the set of lower case letters — these are some of the problems which require investigation. What are the kinds of analogues possible for a fundamental category and what is their increasing order of concreteness — these too are problems to be investigated. In the example given in section 74, the class number will have the structure like the following:

X61.(*z*—).(*s*—):2:N5

76 The Foci in Optional Facets

The foci to follow the lower case letters will, wherever possible, be fixed by the Principle of Consistent Order. If there is no prototype for this principle to follow as we were able to find in the case of the Departmental Facet, the foci may be fixed by the Principle of Evolutionary Order, if it lands itself to application. If it does not, the Principle of Unscheduled Mnemonics may be used to fix the foci.

761 Example

In the example given in section 74, the foci in the different optional facets may be determined as follows: —

In the Denomination Facet, the foci may be fixed in the increasing value of the denomination, reserving 0 for fractions of a rupee, 1 for the single digited denomination and so on. 1,000 being of four digits and the lowest number with four digits, 1,000 may be represented by 41. This is using the Principle of Consistent Order. Thus the focus in the Denomination facet will be z41.

In the Material Facet also, the Principle of Consistent Order can be got more easily by using Subject Device. Since the number for Paper is given as M13 in the chapter M Useful Arts, we fix the focus in this facet as *s*M13.

Thus the number for the Specific Subject in question becomes X61.*z*41.*s*M13:791:2:N5

762 *The Result Aimed At*

The following order of the specific subjects of varying extension, which may arise in documentation work, illustrates the result aimed at in the assembling of entries: —

1. X61	Currency
2. X61::2:N5	Currency in India upto 1950
3. X61:791	Demonetisation
4. X61:791:2:N5	Demonetisation in India upto 1950
5. X61.*s*	Material forms of currency
6. X61.*s*::2:N5	Material forms in India upto 1950
7. X61.*s*M13	Paper currency
8. X61.*s*M13::2:N5	Paper currency in India upto 1950
9. X61.*s*M13:791	Demonetisation of paper currency
10. X61.*s*M13:791:2:N5	Demonetisation of paper currency in India upto 1950
11. X61.*z*	Denominations in currency
12. X61.*z*::2:N5	Denominations in currency in India upto 1950
13. X61.*z*4	Denominations in currency with value in four digits
14. X61.*z*4::2:N5	Denominations in currency with value in four digits in India upto 1950
15. X61.*z*4:791	Demonetisation of currency with value in four digits

16. X61.z4:791:2:N5	Demonetisation of currency with value in four digits in India upto 1950
17. X61.z4.s	Material forms of currency with value in four digits
18. X61.z4.s::2:N5	Material forms of currency with value in four digits in India upto 1950
19. X61.z4.sM13	Paper currency with value in four digits
20. X61.z4.sM13::2:N5	Paper currency with value in four digits in India upto 1950
21. X61.z41	Currency of value of 1000 units
22. X61.z41::2:N5	Thousand rupees currency in India upto 1950
23. X61.z41:791	Demonetisation of currency of value of 1000 units
24. X61.z41:791:2:N5	Demonetisation of currency of Rs. 1000 in India upto 1950
25. X61.z41.s	Material forms of currency of value of 1000 units
26. X61.z41.s::2:N5	Material forms of currency of Rs. 1000 in India upto 1950
27. X61.z41.sM13	Paper currency of value of 1000 units
28. X61.z41.sM13::2:N5	Rs. 1000 notes in India upto 1950
29. X61.z41.sM13:791	Demonetisation of paper currency of value of 1000 units
30. X61.z41.sM13:791:2:N5	Demonetisation of Rs. 1000 notes in India upto 1950

This is only a tentative model to form a concrete basis for stimulating thought on the matter. This does not by any means represent what may be finalised.

77 Facility for Research

These are all still in the stage of conjecture. Considerable experience must be gained to determine if these conjectures are in the domain of practicability and if such prescriptions will generally, if not invariably, lead everybody, who has had the necessary training, to arrive at the same class number for a given subject admitting of one or more optional facets. If they will, they will fall in a fairly helpful order and the symbiosis with the catalogue entries, ensured by chain procedure mentioned in Chapter 5, will provide for alternative helpful orders. And the specialist readers, whose best will be put forth only if they are readily put alongside the microscopic units of thought embodied in articles and not merely the macroscopic masses embodied in books, will be able to get the best possible service in an intrinsically complicated situation. How far will this hope be realised? It can be veryfied only by the actual application of these suggestions. To experiment with these suggestions, considerable opportunity, man-power with leisure for research, finance, and access to specialised libraries where intensive documentation service is needed, valued and sought, are required. It is urged that the learned world and the business world, bodies like the Royal Societies, National Academies and the apical business libraries in all the chief businesses in the different countries, the government departmental libraries in the different countries and foundations of international reach like those of Rockefeller, Carnegie and the Princeton Institute for Advanced Studies should combine together and provide the necessary facilities. I made this appeal in my lecture on *Selfperpetuating classification — its need and possibilities* at a joint meeting of the Aslib and the Society of Visiting Scientists at Old Burlington Street, London on 29 September 1948; and I repeat this appeal through these pages to a still wider audience.

Post-script: The above is an over-simplified approach for demonstration purposes. Since it was written, further investigation has led to the designing of different connecting symbols for the different fundamental categories and to the concept of primordial schedules and signature digits. The results of the investigation in progress are coming out regularly in the *Abgila*, the quarterly organ of the Indian Library Association. Other problems are also indicated in the book *Classification and communication* being brought out as volume 3 of the Library Science Series of the University of Delhi.

Chapter 8

ORGANISATION FOR RESEARCH IN LIBRARY CLASSIFICATION

81 Need for Team-work

What has been said in the preceding chapters implies that team-work on a world-scale is necessary to take library classification to the next stage in its evolution, to make it self-perpetuating and to keep it ever evolving so as to keep step with the evolution in the thought of the learned world and the methods of the business world and to be ever a match to the challenge of the field of knowledge. A work of this nature creates indeed a new region of its own in the field of knowledge This must be recognised by the world. This must be recognised by the library profession itself. If this is recognised there will be no fission in it into librarians and documentalists. This is a region which had not been cultivated properly till now. It has, therefore, the lure of the unknown, the advantages of cultivating virgin soil and also the disadvantages of having to work in an unchartered new terrain. There is no longer need to leave the opening up of new regions to solitary adventurers like Columbus. The world has learned the advantage of organising such a pioneering work as a broad-based permanent project and maintaining for its pursuit, a large team of competent specialists.

811 Cosmic Economy

The whole purpose of providing for specialisation is, from one point of view, to meet the diversified needs of society. This also respects at the same time the specificity of the field of interest and the ~~research~~ capacity of individuals. Cosmic economy is indeed such that the frequency distribution of such specificity and capacity among the members of a normal group answers exactly the diverse needs of the group. The larger the group is, the more close is the correlation. The correlation should be expected to be at its best if the world is taken as a whole. The ills of the world are often traceable to failure in putting the right person in the right place and providing him with the right kind of training and the right kind of facilities for the specific work for which he is best fitted. It is now realised that progress of research in the traditional sciences and technologies and other subjects is retarded by insufficient reference service. This is due to the inefficiency in documentation work. This in its turn is due to absence of provision for research in library classification. It was the realisation of this, vague though it might have been, which led to the Conference convened by the Royal Society in June 1948 and the resolutions passed by it, urging the need for putting up a team for research in library classification and the proper utilisation of the work of that team.

82 *Character of the Team*

The character of the team required is determined by the kinds of specialised functions involved in the construction and maintenance of a classificatory language of ordinal numbers of a relatively long expectation of life and endowed with a large element of self-perpetuation or at least a large capacity for improvement without the need to burn the boat, again and again, and starting afresh. As it has been stated in section 541 of *Classification and international documentation* published in May 1948 as fasc. 4 of volume 14 of the *Review of documentation* of the F.I.D., the team should be made of five subteams: —

(1) The intuitive classificationists;
(2) The intellectual classificationists;
(3) The classifiers;
(4) The reference librarians; and
(5) The specialists in the different formations in the field of knowledge.

83 *Function of the Intuitive Classificationists*

The function of the sub-team of intuitive classificationists is of a fundamental nature. They should be able to relate all possible manifestations in the field of knowledge to a few fundamental patterns. They should isolate phases. They should lay down methods for determining the compulsory and optional facets of several subjects. They should devise delicate objective tests of several subjects. They should prescribe the necessary connective symbols and fix their ordinal values. They should design the digits needed for the base of notation. They should hit upon a happy optimum for the number of digits in the base of notation, so that the average number of digits in class numbers is kept within convenient limits. They should make due provision for anterior and posterior common subdivisions. They should make the determination of the differentiated optional facets depend on mnemonics so as to reduce enumeration to the minimum. The work of the intuitive classificationist of high potency will often be ahead of contemporary thought and practice. The time has come for reducing the time-lag between such work and its correct evaluation. A centre of intuitive, creative men, like the Princeton Institute for Advanced Studies, should include library classification also among the main subjects of its pursuit. It should admit into its circle a good assortment of intuitive classificationists. It is the one place in the world where creative men can blossom to their fullness, unsmothered by many a blight to which they are prone in any other atmosphere. Another advantage of their being entertained in that wonderful Institute, which charmed me when I was there in August 1948, will become obvious in section 87 of this chapter.

84 *Function of the Intellectual Classificationists*

The function of the sub-team of the intellectual classificationists is of an arduous nature. At the rate at which boundaries of knowledge are being extended and criss-cross formations are thrown forth by field of knowledge, there will be constant work to be done by this sub-team. They should keep a vigilant eye on all new formations in the field of knowledge. They should fix the facet-formula for all new specific subjects. They should keep the models for optional facets frequently renewed. They should keep listing the new analogues of Unscheduled Mnemonics manifesting themselves from time to time. They should be distributed in the different national, academic and business libraries in the world and allowed to use them as their laboratories and observation stations. They should be periodically deputed to work and refill themselves in a place like the Princeton Institute for Advanced Studies. They should be men who have had some research experience in some fundamental science and be familiar with the different methods of investigation used in the different regions of the field of knowledge.

85 The Function of the Classifiers

The function of the sub-team of classifiers is of a routine nature. Their normal work is to translate into the classificatory language the names of specific subjects which get embodied in books and articles from day to day. As and when cases appear transcending the capacity of the phase-formulae, the facet-formulae, and the anterior and posterior common subdivisions prescribed, the analogues of the Unscheduled Mnemonics listed and the optional facet groupings provided, the classifiers should bring them to the notice of the sub-team of intellectual classificationists — even as the pilot of an aircraft has to bring to the notice of the ground engineer any extra-ordinary situation that developed during flight.

86 The function of Reference Librarians

The function of the sub-team of reference librarians is like that of public relation officers. It is they that have the fullest chance, every minute of their life, to see the extent to which library classification fulfils itself. They should observe its faults and short-comings as disclosed in the glow of the triple contact between themselves, the reading and kindred materials and their users. The other three sub-teams have only occasional chances to see if the classificatory language they conceive, design and build is maintaining itself library-worthy and service-worthy. The readers themselves do not know what to expect of the library as service. The inadequacy of the service rendered has to be inferred often by the fleeting expression of feeling — often expressed not vocally but by other subtle manifestations. The reference librarians are the only persons who have a chance to observe them, integrate them and trace them to faults in the different parts of the machinery of the library. It is they that are in the best position to advise about the faults so discoverable in library classification. These persons should be men who love humanity and derive their own joy at the sight of the joy appearing on the faces of readers by satisfied wants.

87 The Function of Subject Specialists

The function of the sub-team of the workers in the different regions of the field of knowledge is of a basic nature. It is in their hands that knowledge grows. Myriads of new specific subjects appear and get shaped as a result of their investigation. Each of them should be isolated. Their helpful order should be indicated. The expressive names of each of them in the natural language should be framed. They should help, either directly or through the reference librarians who serve them, the classificationists in their work. It is not so much the routine workers as the creative intuitive thinkers and the advanced intellectual investigators that can be of the greatest help to the intuitive and the intellectual classificationists.

The greatest concentration of first-rate creative souls and gifted intellectuals belonging to the greatest number of regions of knowledge is found today in the Princeton Institute for Advanced Studies. The greatest opportunity for productive co-operation between the first two and the last sub-teams of the team needed to keep the classificatory language ever evolving with the evolution of the field of knowledge will therefore occur in that Institute. This is the reason for the appeal made to that Institute in sections 83 and 84.

88 The Organisation

Library classification is an international language. The more it gets fitted for documentation work at the deeper levels, the more profound it becomes. Moreover the deeper, *i.e.* the more specialised, the region of the field of knowledge, the smaller the number of the workers; the smaller the number of workers, the more scattered they will be in the different linguistic regions of the world; the more linguistically divergent they are, the greater the need for an international language which can assemble together in a helpful, systematic order the nascent thought expressed in the several languages. Again the more scattered the workers in the specialised regions of the field of knowledge, the greater the need for an international basis for the organisation for the maintenance of library classification.

Library Classification and Cataloguing are inseparable; and therefore one and the same organisation must look after library classification and the rules for the catalogue codes, which prescribe subject headings.

Such an organisation is best formed as part of the IFLA and the F.I.D. But these two bodies are too poor to provide the necessary secretariate and the funds to carry on its work. They can only provide the brain-power. Their brain-power can be utilised only if some other international body provides the funds necessary to maintain the secretariate and the publication expenses. In the present set-up of the organisation of the world, the only international body which is designed to take up such a responsibility is the UNESCO. Its Department of Libraries should provide the funds and the secretariate with which the IFLA and F.I.D. can work the international organisation for library classification and cataloguing codes. The Rockefeller and Carnegie Foundations may be able to provide funds for specific projects. The Princeton Institute for Advanced Studies may provide facilities. There are also other problems like the professional training of librarians including documentalists, the co-ordination of abstacting services and the standardisation of library apparatus and technique of all other kinds which need promotion by the IFLA and the F.I.D. with the help of the Department of Libraries of the UNESCO. The amalgamation of the IFLA and the F.I.D. will pool the available brain-power better and avoid the development of contradictory voices by the force of friction and prestige and the confusion caused by such voices in the minds of the public and the UNESCO. If the IFLA and F.I.D. amalgamate and if the UNESCO utilises the professional knowledge thus pooled and provides the necessary finance and the secretariate through its Department of Libraries, we shall get the stablest possible organisation for the maintenance of library classification as an international project — a project which develops it as an international language of ordinal numbers, self-perpetuating in a large measure and meeting with every success in facing the continued challenge of the field of knowledge.

INDEX

1. The reference is to the number of the chapter or section.
2. In a few cases, the reference is to the 'Conspectus' which occurs at the beginning of the book.

d.i.r.t. = described in relation to
i.r.t. = in relation to.
q.i.r.t. = qouted in relation to
r.i.r.t. = referred in relation to